The Joke's on EWE!

Jokes, Riddles & Funny Stories Little David Told His Sheep

The Joke's on EWE!

Jokes, Riddles & Funny Stories
Little David Told His Sheep

Paul M. Miller

BARBOUR
PUBLISHING

© 2006 by Barbour Publishing, Inc.

ISBN 1-59789-125-8

Illustrations © Ken Save

Published by Barbour Publishing, Inc., P.O. Box 719, Uhrichsville, Ohio 44683, www.barbourbooks.com

Our mission is to publish and distribute inspirational products offering exceptional value and biblical encouragement to the masses.

 Member of the
Evangelical Christian
Publishers Association

Printed in the United States of America.

5 4 3 2 1

Contents

Introduction
Who Put the *Ewe* in Humor?

"Has anyone seen David this morning?"

"Yeah, Pop—he's out in the north pasture with his stupid sheep."

"There's nothing dumb about those sheep, son. They just don't have much of a sense of humor, that's all."

"Well, from what I hear, your youngest is trying to rectify that."

Cut to the north pasture. David sits under a sprawling thorn tree, with his harp slung over a low-hanging branch. Lined up in front of him is a row of shaggy sheep who really couldn't care less.

"Okay, so you didn't like that one," admits the shepherd kid, scanning pages in *Solomon's Funniest*. "Here, listen to this one—it'll really crack you up!"

You'd be surprised what a good laugh or two will do for the stuff that ails you. David discovered that his flock particularly liked this one:

What do you call a sheep in a tutu?
A baaa-lerina.

Here's another one that got a lot of snickers:

Are you a wolf in sheep's clothing?
No, I'm just a wolf whose GQ subscription expired.

So maybe you're asking, "Who in the world wants a joke book about sheep?"

To which I would reply, "Ah, come on—there's more than sheep jokes in here. Just thought the title was so great! We call that *marketing*."

You: "Well, I call it baaaaaaad!"

Me: "There ya go. And you thought you were getting fleeced!"

Jesus once said, "Many sheep I have that are not of this fold."

Let's put our own spin on that and say, "Many jokes you'll find here, and they're from everybody's fold." Enjoy them—after all, *The Joke's on Ewe!*

PAUL M. MILLER

1
Shepherds and Their Silly Sheep:
The Flock's Favorites

Father: David! Is that you out there?

David: Yeah, Pop. I'm tuckin' my sheep in for the night. But I don't think little Louie's feeling well—his nose is warm.

Father: That's for dogs, Davy. Not sheep.

David: Oh. Well, I don't think I'll take a chance—better call a *lambulance*!"

A county agent was out checking on farms when he drove by a three-legged chicken. Soon, he noticed that the chicken was running right beside his car. The man stepped on the gas, but at fifty miles an hour the chicken had actually taken a lead. After a few miles, the chicken zipped up a driveway and into a barn behind a farmhouse.

The agent drove up to the house, got out, and knocked on the door. When the man told the farmer what he had just seen, the farmer replied that his son was a geneticist who had developed this breed of chicken so that he and both of his parents could each get a drumstick. The agent beamed. "That's fantastic. How do they taste?"

The farmer scratched his chin and admitted, "I don't know. We can never catch 'em."

~~~~~

Patient: Doctor, sometimes when I wake up in the morning I think I'm Donald Duck, other times I think I'm Mickey Mouse.
Doctor: How long have you had these Disney spells?

How many computer technicians does it take to change a lightbulb?
Three. Two to hold the ladder, and one to screw it into a faucet.

~~~~~

Did you hear about Joey the procrastinator? He didn't get his birthmark until he was eight years old.

~~~~~

Knock, knock.
Who's there?
Control freak. Now you say, "Control freak who?"

~~~~~

Rose: Why not say "288" in a polite conversation?
Lily: Because it's two gross.

~~~~~

Why did Dorothy get lost in Oz?
She had three men giving her directions.

It was Johnny Carson who asked this thought-provoking question: "If airline travel is so safe, how come flight attendants sit right next to the emergency exit?"

~~~~~

Chucky: I just swallowed a frog.
Flossy: Doesn't it make you feel sick?
Chucky: Sick? I'm liable to croak any minute!

~~~~~

Jim: I swim with my head above water.
Kim: Well, of course you do. Wood floats!

~~~~~

"Do you always swim with your socks on?"
"Only when the water's cold."

~~~~~

What has ears but can't hear a thing?
A cornfield.

A man was watching a fisherman at work. The fisherman caught a giant trout but threw it back into the river. Next the fisherman reeled in a huge wide-mouth bass and threw it back. Finally, the fisherman caught a small bass. He smiled and put the little fish in his creel.

"Hey," yelled the guy who was watching. "How come you threw back a giant trout and a huge wide-mouth, and then kept a puny bass?"

The fisherman hollered back, "Small frying pan."

~~~~~

Some advice from eight-year-olds:

- Never trust a dog to watch your food.
- When you want something expensive, ask your grandparents.
- Never smart off to a teacher whose ears are twitching.
- Wear a hat when feeding seagulls.
- Don't ever be too full for dessert.
- Never try to baptize a cat.
- Forget the cake—go for the icing.
- Never spit when riding a roller coaster.

There once was a man from Algiers
Who tried growing corn in his ears.
When the temperature rose,
He leapt to his toes,
Now popping is all that he hears.

~~~~~

How was copper wire invented?
Two misers were arguing over a penny.

~~~~~

The human cannonball decided to retire. The circus owner cried, "But you can't! Where am I going to find another man of your caliber?"

~~~~~

Tutt: Know why the archaeologist was depressed?
Mutt: Why?
Tutt: His career was in ruins.

~~~~~

What did the judge say to his dentist?
Pull my tooth, the whole tooth, and nothing but the tooth.

Sergeant: Private!
Private: Yes, sir!
Sergeant: You failed to show up for camouflage class
    yesterday.
Private: How do you know that, sir?

~~~~

How can you tell you have a slow dog?
He brings you yesterday's newspaper.

~~~~

Benson: Do you like going to work?
Tim: Yes, and I like going home, too. It's the stuff in
    between that I don't like.

~~~~

The Czech man went to the eye doctor to have his
vision tested. The eye chart read, C V K P M W X F
C X. The doctor asked, "Can you read that?"

    The man replied, "Can I read it? I dated her once."

Ginny: Remember my old boy friend Jack? Man, is he rolling in the dough!
Lenny: What's his business?
Ginny: He's a baker.

~~~~~

Pete: My girlfriend's so conceited, she goes to the garden to let the flowers smell her.
Zeke: That's nothing. My girlfriend's so selfish, she won a trip for two to Paris and went twice.

~~~~~

A really bad actor was playing Hamlet. His performance was so terrible that during the "To be or not to be" speech the audience threw their shoes at him. The actor stepped downstage and announced, "Look, folks—I didn't write this junk."

~~~~~

Joe: I have insomnia so bad.
Moe: Really? How bad is it?
Joe: It's so bad the sheep fall asleep.

Susie: My sister is so modest!
Annie: How modest is she?
Susie: She's so modest she goes into a closet to change her mind.

~~~~

Mr. Elf: I watch a lot of television.
Mr. Hobbit: What's your favorite kind of program?
Mr. Elf: Gnome improvement shows.

~~~~

Driver: Does this road lead to Prairie Village?
Kansan: Don't know.
Driver: Well, can you tell me which road I should take to get to Johnson County?
Kansan: Nope.
Driver: You sure don't know much, do you?
Kansan: Maybe not. But I'm not the guy who's lost!

~~~~

Passenger: Driver, does this bus stop at the river?
Driver: Well, if you hear a really big splash, you'll know it doesn't.

A young man went for an interview as a potential guest on a television talk show. "What do you do?" asked the show's producer.

"I imitate birds," the young man answered.

"What?" grumbled the producer. "People who imitate birds are a dime a dozen. Forget it—we can't use you."

"Okay," replied the disappointed young man. Then he flapped his arms and flew out the window.

~~~~~

Zane: Boy, is my father cheap!
Jane: Yeah? How cheap is he?
Zane: He's so cheap he's mad at the doctor because he got better before he finished his medicine.

~~~~~

Lisa: I've heard that a milk bath is good for the skin, so I'll need enough to fill the tub.
Grocer: Pasteurized?
Lisa: No, just up to my chin will do.

Harry: Someday I'd like to ride on a submarine.
Larry: Not me! I wouldn't set foot on any ship that sinks on purpose.

~~~~

Lady: Young man, will you call me a taxi?
Doorman: Certainly, Madam. You are a taxi.

~~~~

Lanny: I can't figure out why it's so hard, Danny, but my wife just doesn't understand me. Does yours?
Danny: I doubt it. She's never even mentioned your name.

~~~~

City slicker, to farmer: Lived here all your life?
Farmer: Not yet.

~~~~

Why did the cow jump over the moon?
The farmer had cold hands.

WANTED: Intelligent watchmaker wishes to contact clockmaker with high IQ for timely discussion.

~~~~~

Tiny: Show me a tough guy and I'll show you a coward.
Bruto: Well, I'm a tough guy!
Tiny: And I'm a coward.

~~~~~

Father: If you kids don't stop making so much noise, I'll go deaf!
Kids: Too late—we stopped an hour ago!

~~~~~

Patient: Doctor! Something's wrong! I'm shrinking!
Doctor: Take it easy, sir. You'll just have to be a little patient.

~~~~~

Don: I plan to beat the inheritance tax.
Ron: How are you going to do that?
Don: I'm going to die broke.

Patient: Nurse, nurse!
Nurse: What is it, sir?
Patient: I keep seeing spots in front of my eyes.
Nurse: Have you seen a doctor?
Patient: No, just spots.

~~~~~

Celebrity: It is so good to be with you wonderful people here at Shady Rest nursing home. Does anyone here know who I am?
Resident: No, but don't worry. Go down to the front desk and they'll tell you.

~~~~~

Judge: Have you ever held up a train?
Outlaw: Now and then.
Judge: Where have you held up trains?
Outlaw: Here and there.
Judge: What things have you taken from passengers?
Outlaw: This and that.
Judge: Sheriff, lock this man up!
Outlaw: Hey! When do I get out of jail?
Judge: Oh, sooner or later.

Did you hear about the candle shop that burned down? Everyone stood around and sang "Happy Birthday."

~~~~~

Father: How did the job interview go?
Trudy: The interviewer told me they had an opening for a person of my ability.
Father: Well, that sounds good.
Trudy: Not exactly. She was referring to the exit.

~~~~~

Scoutmaster: How could you get lost? Didn't you have your compass with you?
Scout: Sure, but the needle kept pointing north, and I wanted to go south.

~~~~~

Mother: I send you out to buy some new clothes, and you come back with a deck of cards.
Son: But Mom, the salesman said I could have four suits for a dollar.

A man walked into his neighborhood coffee shop with a large carrot tucked behind his ear. The girl behind the counter noticed, but decided not to say anything, figuring the guy was just waiting to be asked about it. For thirty straight mornings the man game in wearing a carrot. On the thirty-first day he entered the coffee shop with a banana behind his ear, and the girl behind the counter finally broke down.

"Okay, I give up. Why are you wearing a banana behind your ear?" she asked.

"Couldn't find a carrot today," the man replied.

～～～

Bill: I heard a man jumped off Golden Gate Bridge rather than pay his income tax.
Will: That must have been a debt-defying leap.

～～～

George: Hey, I thought you were going bear hunting.
Lenny: Well, I got as far as the interstate.
George: What happened?
Lenny: I saw a sign that said, BEAR LEFT—so I came home.

Gambler 1: I finally found a foolproof way to come back from Las Vegas with a small fortune.
Gambler 2: Tell me—quick!
Gambler 1: Go there with a large fortune.

~~~~~

Limerick anyone?

A precocious young lady named Lillian
Protruded her tongue at a Chilean;
Her mother said, pleading,
"Remember your breeding,
That trick is distinctly reptilian."

~~~~~

Chemistry teacher: What is the formula for water?
Student: H-I-J-K-L-M-N-O.
Chemistry teacher: What made you give a silly answer like that?
Student: You said it was H to O.

Private: Why are you throwing me out of the Marines, sir?

General: Because you are rotten to the Corps, soldier!

2
Let's Hear It for the *Ewe-S-A:*
Star-Spangled Jokes

Father: Supper's ready, Davy. Wash up and come on in now!

David: Will be right there, Pop. Gotta get two of these critters out of a prickly *Bush*. One of them is very stalwart—he's my *Tru-man* of a lamb. The other one is *Lincoln* his wounds.

Father: Come now, son, I don't want to put a *Nixon* what you're doing—but it's time to *Fillmore* than your sheep with food.

David: Well, sir, I can't af-*Ford* to lose any of these animals. *Grant* me a few more minutes, please.

Father: Well. . .

David: Come on, Pop, lighten up—*J.F.K.*

Father: What's that mean?

David: "Just For Kicks!"

Father: Yeah? Well how about—*F.D.R.*

David: What's that?

Father: Your "Food's Down the Rubbish" disposal!

Here's the reason the French get so unhappy with the U.S.A.: Years ago, they gave us the wonderful croissant—*le cwa-soh*—so what do we do? We turn it into *croissandwich.* Thank you very much.

~~~~~

Jay Leno makes an observation about the food habits of Americans: "Do you remember when they said movie popcorn is bad for you, the same for Chinese food? They now say that sandwiches are bad for you because of the high fat content. Anything with mayo, cheese, or meat is bad for you. Do you realize that all those years when you were a kid and you carried your lunch to school, the Twinkie was probably the healthiest thing in there?"

~~~~~

Lots of small towns in the U.S.A. One of them is Ferguson, Ohio. When you enter the city limits there is a sign that reads, WELCOME TO FERGUSON. BEWARE OF THE DOG. And the all-night drugstore closes at noon.

Did you hear about the LOTS FOR SALE sign that caused a European tourist to ask, "Lots of *what*?"

~~~~~

A kindergarten teacher was showing her class an encyclopedia page illustrating several national flags. She pointed to the American flag and asked, "What flag is this?"

A little girl called out, "That's the flag of our country."

"Very good," the teacher said. "And what's the name of our country?"

" 'Tis of thee," the girl said confidently.

~~~~~

You know that you're from California when. . .

- The fastest part of your commute is down your driveway.
- You were born somewhere else.
- You know how to eat an artichoke.
- You go to a tanning salon before you hit the beach.
- You drive to your neighborhood block party.

If you're from Minnesota, you've heard these before. . . .

- I came, I thawed, I transferred.
- If you love Minnesota, raise your left ski.
- Many are cold, but few are frozen.
- There are only three things you can grow in Minnesota: colder, older, and fatter.
- Land of two seasons: Winter is coming, winter is here.
- Save a Minnesotan—eat a mosquito.

~~~~~

Among other things, what do Americans do?

- We yell for the government to balance the budget; then we take the last dime we have to make the down payment on a car.

- We yell for speed laws that will stop fast driving; then we won't buy a car if it can't go over a hundred miles per hour.

- We get scared to death if we vote a billion dollars for education; then we're unconcerned when we find out we're paying three zillion dollars a year for cigarettes.

- We tie up our dog while letting our sixteen-year-old son run wild.

- We work hard on a farm so we can move into town, where we can make more money—so we can move back to the farm.

- We have more food to eat than any other country in the world—and more diets to keep us from eating it.

- We still get lumps in our throats at the ball game when the "Star-Spangled Banner" is sung.

~~~~~

What are the three great American parties?
Democratic, Republican, and Tupperware.

~~~~~

A pharmacist was giving instructions to a lady at his counter; "Take one capsule three times a day with plenty of water," he said. "This medication can make your skin sensitive, so try to avoid exposure to the sun."

The woman gave him a quizzical look and replied, "You're new here in Oregon, aren't you?"

A young man was running for the senate in New York State. His political advisor heard some news that really upset him.

"Look," he said to his candidate, "you've got to go to Albany right away or you'll lose a lot of votes. They're telling a bunch of lies about you there."

"I've got to go to Buffalo first or I'll lose more votes," the candidate replied.

"What's going on in Buffalo?"

"They're telling the truth about me there!"

~~~~~

Late one hot morning, two northern tourists driving through Louisiana saw on the map the next logical stop for lunch would be a town called Natchitoches. They wondered about the pronunciation, one favoring NATCH-ee-toe-cheese and the other saying it made more sense as Natch-eye-TOTT-chez.

They stopped at a fast food joint and went inside. A fresh-faced girl took their order. One tourist said, "We need somebody local to settle an argument for us. Could you please pronounce where we are. . .very slowly?"

The girl leaned over the counter so they could watch her lips and said as distinctly as she could, "Brrrrrrr, grrrrrrrr, Kiiiiinnnggg."

A highway patrolman from an undesignated southern state pulls a pickup over to the side of the road. The officer walks up to the driver's window and asks, "You got any ID?"

" 'Bout what?"

~~~~~~

Inscribed on tombstones around the country:

LOOKED UP THE ELEVATOR SHAFT
TO SEE IF THE CAR WAS ON THE WAY DOWN.
IT WAS.
(New York)

ONCE I WASN'T
THEN I WAS
NOW I AIN'T AGAIN.
(Ohio)

MY LIFE'S BEEN HARD,
AND ALL THINGS SHOW IT.
I ALWAYS THOUGHT SO,
NOW I KNOW IT.
(Vermont)

HERE LIES THE CLAY OF MICHAEL COOTS,
WHOSE FEET YET OCCUPY HIS BOOTS.
HIS SOUL HAS GONE—WE KNOW NOT WHERE
IT LANDED, NEITHER DO WE CARE.
HE SLIPPED THE JOKER UP HIS SLEEVE
WITH VILE INTENTION TO DECEIVE.
AND WHEN DETECTED, TRIED TO JERK
HIS GUN, BUT DIDN'T GET HIS WORK
IN WITH SUFFICIENT SWIFTNESS, WHICH
EXPLAINS THE PRESENCE HERE OF MITCH.
AT GABRIEL'S TRUMP, IF HE SHOULD WAKE,
HE'LL MIGHTY LIKELY TRY TO TAKE
THE TRUMP WITH THAT SAME JOKER HE
HAD SLEEVED SO SURREPTITIOUSLY,
AND WHICH WE PLACED UPON HIS BIER
WHEN WE CONCEALED HIS BODY HERE.
(Colorado)

UNDERNEATH THIS PILE OF STONES
LIES ALL THAT'S LEFT OF SALLY JONES.
HER NAME WAS BRIGGS, IT WAS NOT JONES,
BUT JONES WAS USED TO RHYME WITH STONES.
(New York)

In memory of Jane Bent,
Who kicked up her heels and away she went.
(Massachusetts)

Under this sod
And under these trees
Lieth the body of Solomon Pease.
He's not in this hole,
But only this pod;
He shelled out his soul
And went up to God.
(Ohio)

This blooming youth in health most fair
To his uncle's mill-pond did repair;
Undressed himself and so plunged in
But never did come out again.
(Vermont)

~~~~~

There was a young lady named Hannah,
Who slipped on a peel of banana.
More stars she espied,
As she lay on her side,
Than are found on the Star-Spangled Banner.

Bill Vaughn in the *Kansas City Star*: "A real patriot is the fellow who gets a parking ticket and rejoices that the system works."

~~~~

The University of Alabama football team played Harvard. At a party after the game, an Alabama player approached a girl and asked, "What school do you go to?"

"Yale," the girl replied.

"Okay, WHAT SCHOOL DO YOU GO TO?"

~~~~

Ghost: Please let me join the Marines.
Recruiter: Why?
Ghost: I want to fright for my country.

~~~~

How many Californians does it take to change a lightbulb?
Seven. One to screw in the bulb and six to share the experience.

Why did the ghost join the U.S. Navy?
He wanted to haunt for buried treasure.

~~~

What do you call a Norwegian car?
A Fjord.

~~~

A Texan was trying to impress a guy from Boston with a graphic account of the heroism at the Alamo. He says, "I guess you don't have many heroes where you come from?"

The man from Boston replies, "Well, sir, have you ever heard of Paul Revere?"

And the Texan says, "Paul Revere? Isn't he the guy who ran for help?"

~~~

An Alaskan was on trial in Anchorage. The judge turned to him and asked, "Where were you on the night of October to April?"

A professor asked a student from Wyoming, "What's the opposite of joy?"

"Sadness," replied the student.

"What's the opposite of depression?"

"Elation."

"And what's the opposite of woe?"

"Giddyup."

~~~~~

Maisie: My brother is so dumb!

Daisy: Why do you say that?

Maisie: He read in a magazine that most accidents happen within two miles of the home.

Daisy: So?

Maisey: So, he moved.

~~~~~

Wife: Wasn't that a lovely performance by the American Ballet Theater?

Husband: I don't understand all that toe dancing. Why don't they just get taller girls?

How many New Yorkers does it take to change a lightbulb?
Five. One to change the bulb and four to protect him from muggers.

~~~~~

A sweet little old lady was sitting directly behind the bus driver on a journey from Miami. After fifteen minutes, she tapped the driver on the shoulder and asked, "Are we at Orlando yet?"

He said, "No, lady, I'll tell you when we are."

Fifteen minutes later, she tapped him on the shoulder. "Are we at Orlando yet?"

"No, lady," he snapped. "I'll tell you when we are."

This went on every fifteen minutes, so that by the time they reached Orlando, the driver was close to throttling her. And so it was with great delight that he announced, "This is Orlando. Out you go, lady."

"Oh, no," she said. "I'm going all the way to Jacksonville. It's just that before we left, my daughter told me that when we get to Orlando, I should take my blood pressure pill."

How many Hollywood movie directors does it take to change a lightbulb?
One, but he's going to want to do it fifteen times more.

~~~~~

Father: What should you do when you see the American flag waving?
Little girl: Wave back?

~~~~~

An American and an Irishman met at a farming convention in Kilkenny. The American owned a huge farm back in Texas, while the Irish farmer had no more than a couple of acres outside of Wexford.

"Tell me about your farm," said the Irishman.

"It's enormous," began the Texan, "the biggest farm you ever did see in your life. It stretches halfway across the country. Do you know, I can get in my truck first thing in the morning, drive around my land, and still not cover it all by sunset."

"To be sure," responded the Irishman, "I used to have a truck like that."

"California is a fine place to live, if you happen to be an orange." Fred Allen

~~~~

Cindy: I've been calling and calling the city council to do something about those terrible potholes! After months of badgering, they finally took action.
Mindy: And now are the potholes filled?
Cindy: No, now the city council has an unlisted number!

~~~~

Teacher: Can anyone tell me why the Capitol in Washington has a rotunda?
Student: So our politicians can run around in circles.

~~~~

One day a courageous U.S. mail deliverer was greeted by a boy and a huge dog. The mailman said to the boy, "Does your dog bite?"

"No, sir," replied the boy.

Just then the huge dog bit the mailman.

"Hey," he yelled, "I thought your dog doesn't bite!"

"He doesn't" answered the boy, "but that's not my dog!"

Reporter: What happened to the mouse that was sent to Congress?

Senator: He was just named Squeaker of the House.

~~~~

How many federal employees does it take to screw in a lightbulb?

Sorry, that item has been cut from the budget.

~~~~

Politician: Do you know what made George Washington such a great president?

Interviewer: Sure, he never blamed any of the country's problems on the previous administration.

~~~~

My sister gave me a fabric calendar. Took me three hours to sew in a dental appointment.

~~~~

Boise: Is Helena Nome?

Montana: Idaho, Alaska.

When American products go overseas, the slogans that go with them are often not appropriate in the new languages. The Chevy Nova never sold well in Spanish-speaking countries. *No va* means "It does not go" in Spanish.

When Pepsi started marketing its products in China, the English slogan "Pepsi brings you back to life" was translated quite literally, "Pepsi brings your ancestors back from the grave."

Coca-Cola faced the same issue in China. The characters used to write, *Coca-Cola*, meant "Bite the wax, tadpole." They later selected characters that read, "Happiness in the mouth."

~~~~~

Sal: I know a carpenter who is running for Congress.
Hal: Is he a good politician?
Sal: No, but he built a great campaign platform.

~~~~~

Senator: The U.S. has made a lot of progress over the past hundred years or so.
Reporter: It sure has. President Washington couldn't tell a lie, and now every politician in Washington can.

Patient: Doc, I'm calling long distance from Peculiar, Missouri. I've been on this exercise program of yours for ten days now, and it's just not working.

Doctor: I told you to run five miles a day. Haven't you lost any weight?

Patient: Oh sure, I've lost weight, but now I'm fifty miles from home!

~~~~~

An Irishman walks into a 7-Eleven in Oak Harbor, Washington, and asks the young clerk, "What's the quickest way to get to Coupeville?"

"Are you walking or driving?"

"Driving," replies the man.

"That's the quickest way," says the clerk.

~~~~~

Farmer: Hey, neighbor—you can't take your sheep home that way.

Neighbor: I was just taking a shortcut across your frozen pond. What's wrong with that?

Farmer: Nobody pulls the wool over my ice.

Mr. Montana: You know, I'm quite a catch! My boss says I have a lot of get-up-and-go.

Ellie: Oh yeah? Prove it!

~~~~~

Trevor: There is one word that you Americans always pronounce wrong.

Hank (defensively): What word is that?

Trevor: *Wrong*.

~~~~~

Beach: How ya dune?

Ocean: Just swell!

~~~~~

How is an Idaho potato farmer like a baseball fan?
One yanks roots; the other roots for the yanks.

~~~~~

Why are you always welcome in the Show Me State?
Because Missouri loves company.

Only in America. . .

- How come you never see the headline PSYCHIC WINS LOTTERY?

- If every man were as true to his country as he is to his God, we'd be in a lot of trouble.

- Ever go to an average-man's hospital? Sometimes there's a sign over the emergency room door that reads, TIME HEALS ALL WOUNDS.

- Doesn't it bother you when people litter? Their most creative rationale for throwing an apple core out the car window is, "It will plant seeds for other trees to grow." And, of course, our highways are lined with apple trees—right next to the cigarette-butt bushes.

- What a tragedy: An Amish man in Lancaster County was arrested because the red lantern on the back of his buggy blew out. When he was taken to jail, he was told he could make one phone call. But who was he to call? None of his friends or family has telephones.

- It's been said that the state of Michigan's legislature has passed a law allowing the blind to hunt deer. The biggest supporters of the new law? The deer.

- Joined a health club last year, spent four hundred dollars. Haven't lost a pound. Apparently you gotta show up.

~~~~~

Our town is so small that. . .

- The city limits signs are both on the same post.
- The city jail is called amoeba—it only has one cell.
- Our McDonald's only has one arch.
- The 7-Eleven is a 3½-5½.
- Our one-block long Main Street dead-ends in both directions.
- Second Street is over in the next town.
- Our zip code is a fraction.

3

David, Quit Your Harping!
Jokes about Music and Entertainment

Father: Davy, what kind of music do you play for your sheep?

David: Well, it depends on their mood. They really like my versions of "Harp the Herald Angels Sing" and "Sheep May Safely Graze" by J.S. Baach. But my all-time favorite is "Old Flocks at Home"!

What's wooly and plays really cool music?
A Dixie Lamb Band.

~~~~~

An uppity hostess was talking to one of her guests as the two sat listening to a cello recital.

"Beautiful, isn't it?" asked the hostess.

"Pardon," said the guest.

"I said, it's beautiful, isn't it?"

"I'm sorry," yelled the guest, "I can't hear a thing for that lousy cello!"

~~~~~

When the orchestra began selections from Tschai-kovsky's *Romeo and Juliet*, a woman noticed tears streaming down the cheeks of an elderly man sitting next to her. Before long he was sobbing as if his heart would break.

"You must be an incurable romantic," she whispered to him.

"Not at all," he gulped. "I'm a musician."

What television channel do horses watch?
HayBC

~~~

A ten-year-old boy was practicing his violin at home and the horrible noise was making his dog howl. Upstairs, the boy's father was attempting to read the evening paper. After putting up with the combined racket of screeching violin and howling dog for twenty minutes, the father finally yelled, "Tommy! Can't you play something the dog doesn't know?"

~~~

Chuck: My doctor said I had to give up playing the drums.
Cluck: Why?
Chuck: He lives in the apartment below me.

~~~

Nan: What's green and sings?
Ann: What?
Nan: Elvis Parsley

What do you get if you cross MTV with flowerbeds?
Rock gardens.

~~~~

What happens when you drop a grand piano into a coal mine?
You get A-flat minor.

~~~~

What do you call two bees, a hornet, and a wasp that play violins?
A sting quartet.

~~~~

Betty: My son's majoring in music at college. He plays the tuba.
Lettie: Is he any good?
Betty: Good? Why, he's graduating Magna Cum Loud!

~~~~

"I hate music, especially when it's played."
Jimmy Durante

What's Beethoven doing now?
Decomposing.

~~~~~

Harry: Hey, Larry! Nice trumpet you've got there.
Larry: I borrowed it from my neighbor.
Harry: I didn't know you played the trumpet.
Larry: I can't. And now, neither can my neighbor.

~~~~~

Why can't you go to the bathroom at a Beatles reunion concert?
There's no John.

~~~~~

Bert: Why do you keep singing the same song over and over?
Gert: The melody haunts me.
Bert: That's because you're murdering it!

Fred: I come from a musical family.
Peggy: I never knew that.
Fred: Oh yes, Dad drummed his fingers, Aunt Mae blew her nose, and Grandpa fiddled with his mustache.

~~~~~

What's the difference between a banjo and a lawnmower?
You can tune a lawnmower!

~~~~~

How come those musicians perspire so much?
They must be a sweat band.

~~~~~

Mozart: What did the Terminator say to Beethoven?
Brahms: Tell me.
Mozart: "I'll be Bach!"

What was the cave girl's answer, when asked why she was hitting a boulder with a stick?
"I want to hear some rock music."

~~~~~

What's the name of a donkey who sings classical music?
Braytoven.

~~~~~

Lisa: I once sang the "Star-Spangled Banner" for three
    hours straight.
Ben: Big deal. I sang the "Stars and Stripes Forever."

~~~~~

A man's wife was upset. "Why do you always go out on the patio whenever I sing? Don't you like to hear me?"

"It's not that," responded the husband, "I just want the neighbors to see I'm not beating you!"

Following a late-night gig, an accordion player woke up in the morning and realized he'd left his accordion on the back seat of his car parked out in the street. Convinced that the instrument was probably stolen overnight, he jumped out of bed in his pajamas and dashed out to his car. Sure enough, he discovered that the rear window of his car had been smashed. But when he looked into the back seat, he saw not only his accordion, but two more accordions.

~~~~~

Fred: Don't you wish life were like television?
Ted: I can't answer that now.
Fred: Why not?
Ted: I'm on a commercial break.

~~~~~

Jan: Have you heard of the new diet for guitar players?
Fran: No, what is it?
Jan: It's called the Chet Atkins diet. All you do is
    pick at your food.

What cat is a really famous rock star?
Mewdonna.

~~~~~

Mozart: Did you hear about the glue salesman who became a star singer?
Bach: How?
Mozart: He stuck with it!

~~~~~

Why don't fish watch television?
They don't want to get hooked on it.

~~~~~

What does a funny train ride on?
A laugh track.

~~~~~

Who lives underground and loves to paint?
Vincent Van Gopher.

Why do hummingbirds hum?
Because they can't remember the words.

~~~~~

Patient: Doctor, I was playing the flute when I suddenly swallowed it.

Doctor: Well, let's look on the bright side. You could have been playing the piano.

~~~~~

How many country musicians does it take to screw in a lightbulb?

Five. One to do it, and four to sing about how much they're going to miss the old one.

~~~~~

A woman walked into a music store and asked about a used piano. "This one here must be very old. The keys are all yellow."

"No, the piano isn't that old," said the salesman. "It's just that the elephant was a heavy smoker."

How many folk musicians does it take to screw in a lightbulb?
Forty. One to do it and thirty-nine to complain that it's electric.

~~~~~

How many opera divas does it take to change a lightbulb?
None is needed. Each believes she is the brightest light that illuminates any theater stage.

~~~~~

What do you say to a musical hitchhiker with one leg?
Hip-hop in!

~~~~~

Director: Now, in this scene you jump off the cliff.
Actor: But suppose I get killed?
Director: Don't worry—it's the last scene in the film.

Why did the chicken cross the road?
To get away from the drum recital.

~~~~~

Why do elephants trumpet?
They don't know how to play the violin.

~~~~~

Tommy: My brother has been playing the guitar for
   ten years now.
Molly: He must be pretty good.
Tommy: Not really. It took him nine years to find out
   that he wasn't supposed to blow through it.

~~~~~

Carl: My upstairs neighbors are so loud. Yesterday
   they were banging on the floor all night.
Karl: Did they wake you?
Carl: No. Fortunately I was playing my tuba.

~~~~~

I love the opera. You can't sleep at home like that.

What comes after a tuba?
A three-ba.

~~~~~

Why do bagpipers walk so fast when they play?
To get away from the noise.

~~~~~

Teacher: Scientists believe that cavemen made the first music by banging stones together.
Elvis: Gee, that must have been the first rock music.

~~~~~

"I don't like country music, but I don't mean to denigrate those who do. And for people who like country music, denigrate means 'put down.'"
Bob Newhart

~~~~~

"I like hip-hop. I'm working with Ice Cube, Ice-T, and Herb Tea. I'm changing my name to Snapple."
Accredited to Paul Mooney

Did you know Mozart had no arms and no legs? I've seen statues of him on people's pianos.

~~~~~

Luigi: What did the pianist do when he accidentally glued his hands together?
Ludwig: What?
Luigi: He played by ear.

~~~~~

What do you call a guy who hangs out with musicians?
A drummer.

~~~~~

Producer: Didn't you write a successful play named *The Firefly*?
Writer: Yes, it got glowing reviews.

~~~~~

What's large, gray, and sings calypso?
Harry Elephante.

What did the opera singer say to the unexpected guest?
If Aida known you were Carmen, I'd have made something to Nibeling.

~~~~~

A cub reporter was sent to the circus to do a feature on the sideshow. When he knocked on the door of the midget's trailer, it was opened by an extremely tall man, well over six feet.

"Uh, I'm looking for Shorty O'Brian, circus midget?" asked the reporter.

"I'm Shorty," the tall man answered.

"But. . .you're so tall!" stammered the reporter.

"I know," replied Shorty. "It's my day off."

4

Funnier than the *Wool Street Journal*: Money and Business Jokes

Father: I've been wondering, David, if your flock of sheep is profitable.

David: Well that depends on the Baa Jones Average.

Father: Well, are they Bulls or Bears, Davy?

David: Pop, they're sheep!

Mary: Know what? I never worry about money.
Barry: How come?
Mary: What's the sense in worrying about something I don't have?

~~~~~

Invest in a dairy farm! You'll have plenty of liquid assets!

~~~~~

Wife: Do you love me just because my father left me a fortune?
Husband: Not at all, darling. I would love you no matter who left you the money.

~~~~~

Glamour girl: My face is my fortune.
Agent: Well, you're facing bankruptcy!

~~~~~

How was copper wire discovered?
Two lawyers were arguing over a penny.

Gracie: How much are these oranges?
Grocer: Two for a quarter.
Gracie: How much for just one?
Grocer: Fifteen cents.
Gracie: Fine, then I'll take the other one.

~~~~~

A man was praying to God. He said, "God?"

God responded, "Yes?"

The guy said, "Can I ask a question?"

"Go right ahead," God said.

"God, what is a million years to you?"

God answered, "A million years to me is only a second."

"Hmmm," the man considered. Then he asked, "God, what are a million dollars worth to you?"

God quickly answered, "A million dollars to me is as a penny."

So the man quickly said, "God, can I have a penny?"

And God said, "Sure! Just a second."

~~~~~

I've got a terrific idea for saving money. I borrow a little every month and set it aside!

Rudy: Does money really talk?
Judy: It does to me. Every time I go to the mall my
    cash says, "Good buy! Good buy!"

~~~~~

A kid swallowed a coin and it got stuck in his throat.
His mother yelled for help. A man passing by hit
him in the small of the back, and the coin popped
out.

"I don't know how to thank you, Doctor...," the
boy's mother started.

"I'm not a doctor, ma'am," the man explained,
"I'm from the IRS."

~~~~~

An economist is someone who didn't have the
personality to become an accountant. It was a con-
servative and boring economist who was lecturing
to a college class when he saw that one of his students had fallen asleep. Making a fist, the economist
pounded on the table, which in turn awoke the star-
tled student, who responded, "Cut taxes and reduce
government spending."

Scotty: Are you a lawyer?
Attorney: Yes.
Scotty: How much do you charge?
Attorney: A hundred dollars for four questions.
Scotty: Isn't that awfully expensive?
Attorney: Yes. What's your fourth question?

~~~~~

Financier: Young man, you've asked me for a dollar every morning for the last six months. Why don't you just hit me up for a hundred dollars and get it over with?
Panhandler: It seems imprudent to put all one's begs in one ask it.

~~~~~

Panhandler: How about a quarter, mister?
Passerby: Don't you know panhandling's illegal here?
Panhandler: I'm not panhandling. I'm just practicing my hobby.
Passerby: Your hobby? What's that?
Panhandler: Coin collecting.

"Just about the time you think you can make ends meet, someone moves the end."
Terry Hughes

~~~~~

A man walked into a bank and asked to borrow the sum of two thousand dollars for three weeks. The loan officer asked what collateral the man had. The borrower replied, "I've got a Rolls-Royce. Keep it until the loan is paid off. Here are the keys."

So the loan officer arranged for the car to be driven into the bank's underground parking for safekeeping and gave the borrower two thousand dollars.

Three weeks later, the man walked back into the bank, paid back the two thousand dollar loan plus ten dollars interest, and regained possession of his Rolls-Royce. The loan officer was mystified: "Tell me, sir," he said, "why would someone who drives a Rolls-Royce need to borrow two thousand dollars?"

The borrower smiled and replied, "I had to go abroad for three weeks—where else could I store a Rolls-Royce for that length of time for ten dollars."

A young woman went to cash a check from her husband. The bank cashier asked her to endorse it. So she wrote on the back, "My husband is a wonderful man."

~~~~~

Among the things that money can't buy, is what it used to.

~~~~~

"Americans are getting stronger. Twenty years ago it took two people to carry in ten dollars worth of groceries. Today, a five-year-old can do it."
Henny Youngman

~~~~~

One CEO always scheduled staff meetings for four thirty on Friday afternoons. When one of the employees finally got up the nerve to ask why, the CEO explained, "I'll tell you why—it's the only time of the week when none of you seems to want to argue with me."

An upper mobile young man was just opening the door of his BMW, when a car came along and hit the door, ripping it clean off its hinges. When the police arrived at the scene, the young man was complaining bitterly about the damage to his BMW.

"Officer, look what has been done to my Beeeeeemer," he whined.

"You yuppies are so materialistic, you make me sick!" retorted the officer. "You're so worried about your stupid BMW that you didn't even notice that your left arm has been torn off!"

"Oh my goodness," replied the yuppie, finally noticing the left shoulder where his arm had been, "Where's my Rolex?"

~~~~

I just had plastic surgery. They cut up my credit card.

~~~~

A study of economics usually reveals that the best time to buy anything is last year.

The best things in life are free. And the cheesiest things in life are free with a paid magazine subscription.

~~~~~

Walking through Chinatown, a tourist was fascinated by all the Chinese restaurants, businesses, and signs. He was especially curious about the sign LARS OLAFFSEN'S LAUNDRY.

So he walks into the shop and asks the ancient Chinese gentleman behind the counter, "How did this shop get the name Lars Olaffsen's Laundry?"

The old man answered, "It's the owner's name."

The tourist pressed further. "Well, where or who is the owner?"

"I'm the owner. I'm right here," replied the old man.

"You? How did you get a name like Lars Olaffsen?"

"Simple," answers the old man. "Many years ago when I came to this country, I was in line at the documentation center. The man in front of me was a big tall Swede. The lady looked at him and asked, 'What's your name?' He said, 'Lars Olaffsen.' Then she looked at me and said, 'What's your name?' I said, 'Sem Ting.' "

Advice: The safest way to double your money is to fold it over once and put it back in your wallet.

~~~~~

It was the worst winter in living memory. Thousands of homes were cut off by deep snowdrifts, including a family in a remote mountain cabin in Canada. After three months with no contact with the outside world, the family became the target of a Red Cross rescue team. But for weeks even the Red Cross team couldn't manage to force their way through to the cabin, which by now was almost completely submerged in snow. Finally the brave rescuers succeeded in hacking out a path to the front door of the cabin. Not knowing what they would find, they knocked on the front door. The father answered the door.

"Red Cross," said the team leader.

"Sorry," said the father. "It's been such a tough winter that I don't think we can give anything this year."

~~~~~

"I've been rich and I've been poor. Rich is better."
Mark Twain

Misers are no fun to live with, but they make great ancestors.

~~~~

A nice young postal worker was sorting letters, when she found one addressed as follows:

GOD

c/o Heaven

Upon opening the envelope, she found that the letter enclosed was written by a little old lady who had never asked for anything her whole life long. She was desperately in need of one hundred dollars, and wondered if God could send her the money.

The postal employees were genuinely moved by the request, so they passed the hat. They could only raise ninety dollars, but sent it off anyway.

A few weeks later another letter arrived addressed to God, so the young lady opened it. The letter read, "Thank you for the money, God, I deeply appreciate it. However, I received only ninety dollars. It must have been the no-goods at the post office. I've never trusted them."

Just for fun for accountants:

What's an auditor?
Someone who arrives after the battle, and bayonets all the wounded.

What's an accountant's idea of trashing a hotel room?
Refusing to fill out the guest-comment card.

What's the definition of an accountant?
Someone who solves a problem you didn't know you had in a way you don't understand.

Old accountants never die. They just lose their balance.

5
Mary Had a Little Lamb (Chop):
Jokes about Eating

Father: The larder's getting pretty empty. Maybe we ought to slaughter one of your sheep, Davy.

David: Ah, Pop, we can't do that. They're like my children.

Father: Well, pretty soon they're going to have fuller stomachs than we have.

David: Why don't I go for takeout—Chinese, maybe?

Father: Chinese food? Oh my, I probably won't see you back here for three years or more!

Mary Had a Little Lamb (Chop)

Customer: Waiter, I see a bee in my soup!
Waiter: Of course U-C-A-B! It's alphabet soup.

~~~~~

Tillie: I just crossed a pastry chef with a soft drink.
Millie: What did you get?
Tillie: Baking soda!

~~~~~

What do you get if you cross rice cereal with a kangaroo?
Snap! Crackle! Hop!

~~~~~

Waiter (calling after a departing diner): Hey! What
    about a tip?
Exiting diner: Oh, sorry, here's your tip—don't ever
    eat here!

~~~~~

Lisa: Why did the tomato blush?
Tim: Because it saw the salad dressing.

A sailor named Albert was fat.
His crew and his girl friends knew that.
When asked why he ate
All his food plus the plate,
The sailor weighed anchor and sat.

~~~~~

Two college students were talking about cooking. "I got a cookbook a couple of years ago," said one, "but I couldn't do anything with it."

"Was it too impractical?" asked her friend.

"Absolutely! Every one of the recipes began the same way—'Take a clean dish.'"

~~~~~

When a small boy and his mother came home from shopping at the grocery store, the kid pulled a box of animal crackers out of the bag and emptied them onto the counter.

"What are you doing, Bobby?" asked his mom.

The boy answered, "Well, the box says you can't eat them if the seal is broken. I'm looking for the seal."

Wife: The two things I cook best are meat loaf and apple pie.
Husband: Which is this?

~~~~~

Ben: Why did the raisin go out with a prune?
Donna: Why?
Ben: Because he couldn't find a date.

~~~~~

What's fifty meters high and made of dough?
The Leaning Tower of Pizza.

~~~~~

Boy: Are caterpillars good to eat?
Father: I've told you before, don't talk about such things at the table when we're eating.
Mother: Why do you ask, son?
Boy: 'Cuz I saw one on Daddy's lettuce. Now it's gone.

A family was given a juicy cut of venison by a hunter friend. The wife cooked the deer steaks and served them for dinner.

"What is this," asked the young daughter. "Is it beef?"

"No," said the father.

"Is it pork?" asked their young son.

"No," said the father. "I'll give you a hint. It's what mom sometimes calls me."

"Spit it out, sis!" hollered the boy. "We're eating donkey!"

～～～

The remarkable thing about my mother is that for thirty years she served nothing but leftovers. The original meal was never found.

～～～

Diner: Do you take orders to go?
Waiter: Certainly.
Diner: Then go!

Tory: What's Snow White's favorite drink?
Lori: 7-Up!

~~~~

Diner: Waiter, there's a footprint in my breakfast!
Waiter: Well, you ordered an egg omelet and told me
    to step on it!

~~~~

A hamburger walked into a juice bar, climbed up onto
a stool, looked at the waitress, and ordered a strawberry
smoothie. The waitress looked at the hamburger for a
moment and replied, "I'm sorry sir, but I can't sell you
that smoothie." The hamburger thought about this for
a second, then said, "I can pay for it." After looking
at the hamburger for another moment, the waitress
replied, "I'm sorry, we don't serve food here."

~~~~

Diner: Waiter! This beef steak tastes like an asphalt
    shingle!
Waiter: Sorry, sir, meat prices have gone through the
    roof!

You read it here: Rumor has it that Pringles' original intention was to make tennis balls. But the day the rubber was supposed to arrive, they got a big load of potatoes instead.

~~~~~

If carrots are so good for our eyes, how come we see so many dead rabbits on the highway?

~~~~~

Wouldn't it be cool if you could eat good food with bad food and the good food would cover for the bad food when it got to your stomach? Like you could eat a broccoli spear with an onion ring and they would travel down to your stomach. When they got there the broccoli would say, "It's cool, he's with me."

~~~~~

Did you hear about the new restaurant that just opened on the moon? Good food, but no atmosphere.

A guy walks into restaurant and orders eggs.

The waitress asked, "How would you like those eggs cooked?"

The guy said, "Hey, that would be great!"

~~~~~

Diner: Waiter, your menu plainly states "country fresh eggs." Well, let me tell you, mister, these eggs aren't fresh. And I'd like to know what country they're from.

Waiter: They're from the old country.

~~~~~

Diner: How hot are your tamales?

Waiter: Well, if more than three people eat them at the same time, the sprinkler system goes off.

~~~~~

A guy in a restaurant hollers out, "Hey, there's a fly in my soup."

The waiter replies, "It's possible. The cook used to be a tailor."

Shopper: These turkeys in your frozen food section seem so small. Do they get any bigger?
Grocer: No ma'am. They're dead.

~~~~~

Teacher: Eskimos usually eat whale meat and blubber.
Student: I'd blubber, too, if I had to eat whale meat.

~~~~~

A waiter brings the customer the steak he ordered with his thumb over the meat.

"Are you crazy?" yelled the customer, "you have your hand on my steak."

"What?" answers the waiter. "You want it to fall on the floor again?"

~~~~~

A beggar walked up to a well-dressed woman shopping on Rodeo Drive and said, "I haven't eaten anything in four days."

The woman looked at him and said, "Oh, my, I wish I had your willpower."

Mary Had a Little Lamb (Chop)

Know what you call a nervous hot dog?
A frank-fretter.

~~~~~

Why did the soda-pop bottle go to college?
He wanted to be a fizz ed teacher.

~~~~~

Never forget: Food is an important part of a balanced diet.

~~~~~

Billy: I trained my dog not to beg at the table.
Willy: How did you do that?
Billy: I let him taste my cooking.

~~~~~

Did you know that some people think that eating garlic and onions cuts your risk for some kinds of cancer? Of course, you may lose all your friends.

The top five signs you're a lousy cook:

5. Your family automatically heads for the table every time they hear the smoke alarm.
4. Your kids know what "peas porridge in the pot nine days old" tastes like.
3. Your kids' favorite smoothie is Pepto-Bismol.
2. No matter what you do, the gravy still turns bright purple.
1. You burned the house down trying to make jelly.

~~~~~

How does the man in the moon eat his food?
In satellite dishes.

~~~~~

Mary: Can you eat with chopsticks?
Harry: No. Can you?
Mary: Sure. I even have my own set; they have my initials at one end, and Velcro at the other.

Colorful Mark Twain once remarked, "Sacred cows make the best hamburgers."

~~~~~~

There is a young woman named Lisa
Who can whip up a tasty cheese pizza.
Be it deep dish or crisp,
This will-o'-the-wisp,
Won't let on that she nuked it with ease-a.

~~~~~~

Diner: For an appetizer, I'll take the caviar, but make sure it's imported.

Waiter: Yes, sir.

Diner: Now, don't forget—it must be imported!

Waiter: I understand.

Diner: I will only accepted the caviar if it's imported.

Waiter: Sir, why are you so concerned that I bring you caviar that's imported?

Diner: Because, *I* can't tell the difference.

What is the best thing to eat for your eyesight?
Seafood!

~~~~~

A man walks into his doctor's office. He has a cucumber up his nose, a carrot in his left ear, and a banana in his right ear.

"What's the matter with me?" he asks the doctor.

"You're not eating properly."

~~~~~

Did you hear the joke about oatmeal?
It's a lot of mush.

~~~~~

Bert: Want some ice cream, Ernie?
Ernie: Sure-bert.

~~~~~

The Green Giant was an original member of the peas corps.

Why do people dip bread in melted cheese?
Because it's fonduing it.

~~~~~

Why did the man frown and stare at the can of orange juice?
Because it says "concentrate."

What did the mother ghost tell her baby ghost when he ate too fast?
"Stop goblin your food."

~~~~~

What do you get when you put three ducks in a box?
A box of quackers.

~~~~~

What did the hungry computer eat?
Chips, one byte at a time.

What did one knife say to the other knife?
Look sharp!

~~~~~

Why do fish avoid the computer?
So they don't get caught in the Internet.

~~~~~

Definitions:

* *Oil slick*—What's left on your plate after eating in the school cafeteria.
* *Toxic waste*—Your sister's cooking.
* *Cold front*—What you get when you stand in front of an open refrigerator too long.
* *The Big Dipper*—Someone you don't want to get behind at an all-you-can-eat buffet.
* *Appeal*—What a banana is wrapped in.
* *Assault*—What you use with a pepper.

Mary Had a Little Lamb (Chop)

Little Johnny and his family lived in the country and, as a result, seldom had guests for dinner. On this particular evening, he was eager to help his mom when Dad brought two guests home from work.

When the dinner was nearly over, Little Johnny went to the kitchen and proudly carried in the first piece of apple pie, giving it to his father, who passed it on to a guest.

Little Johnny came in with a second piece of pie and gave it to his father, who again passed it on to a guest.

This was too much for Little Johnny, who said, "It's no use, Dad, the pieces are all the same size."

~~~~~

"Why do you eat so fast?"
"*I want to eat as much as possible before I lose my appetite.*"

Diet Rules:

1. If you eat something and no one sees you eat it, it has no calories.
2. If you drink a diet soda with a candy bar, the calories in the candy bar are canceled out by the diet soda.
3. When you eat with someone, the calories don't count if you don't eat more than he or she does.
4. Foods such as hot chocolate, pancakes, and Sara Lee Cheesecake used for medicinal purposes never count.
5. If you fatten up everyone else around you, then you look thinner.
6. Movie-related food, such as Milk Duds, buttered popcorn, Junior Mints, Red Hots, and Tootsie Rolls are okay to eat, because you do it in the dark.
7. Cookie pieces contain no calories. The process of breaking causes calorie leakage.
8. Stuff licked off knives and spoons have no calories if you are preparing something to eat.
9. Foods of the same color—like spinach and pistachio ice cream—have the same number of calories.
10. Chocolate is a universal color, and may be substituted for any other food color.

Mary Had a Little Lamb (Chop)

What's an astronaut's favorite sandwich?
Launch meat.

~~~~~

Mickey: What do cats call mice on skateboards?
Minnie: I haven't the slightest idea.
Mickey: "Meals on Wheels."

~~~~~

What did the left eye say to the right eye?
Between us, something smells.

~~~~~

What starts with "t" ends with "t" and is filled with "t"?
A teapot.

~~~~~

What do you call cheese that is not yours?
Nacho cheese!

Army doctor: You're looking pale, Corporal. When did you eat last?

Corporal: 1959, sir.

Army doctor: What? How could your survive so long?

Corporal: Well, sir, it's only 2130 now.

~~~~~

How do you kill tortellini?

Spray them with pastacide.

~~~~~

Martha Stewart didn't suggest these. . .

- For a real St. Patrick's Day treat, leave the corned beef out on the counter for a few days beforehand. You not only get the taste of the corned beef, but it will provide a festive shade of holiday green to your holiday table.
- Your screen door can double as a handy cheese grater.
- In a pinch, frozen water can substitute for ice.

The top ten reasons we are overweight:

10. Hey, we get eighty channels of great television twenty-four hours a day. There's no time to exercise.
9. Girl Scout Cookies get better every year.
8. The colossal failure of Salad King drive-thru franchise.
7. Just to spite Richard Simmons.
6. Addition of a diet soda does NOT mean your bacon cheeseburger/chili fries combo is a healthy meal.
5. We are still unconvinced that it's not really butter.
4. Fashion models are not good examples of real American women for our little girls.
3. Slim Fast tastes better with a scoop of Ben & Jerry's.
2. One word: Sprinkles!

And the number-one reason why we are overweight:

1. "Did somebody say McDonald's?"

What can't you eat for breakfast?
Lunch and dinner.

~~~~~

Waiter: May I take your order?
Diner: Yes, I'm just wondering, how do you prepare your chickens?
Waiter: Nothing special, ma'am. We just tell them straight out that they're going to die.

~~~~~

Jason (entering a restaurant): Do you serve crabs here?
Waiter: Yes, sir, we'll serve just about anybody.

6

Ewe, Me, and the Rest of the Flock:
Family Jokes

Father: I hear a ewe gave birth last night. We should celebrate.

David: Yeah. Effie, that's her name, is so happy. And Clarence, he's the proud father, is passing out cigars to the rest of the flock.

Father: Davy, do you think that's a healthy thing to do? I mean, the Hebrew Medical Association has...

David: Ah, Pop, not to worry—they're exploding cigars. Only problem, the new baby isn't getting much sleep.

A teenage girl had to stay at her girlfriend's overnight. She was unable to call her parents until the next morning.

"Mom, it's Caroline. I'm fine. My car broke down last night, by the time I got to Julie's house it was well past midnight. I knew it was too late to call. Please don't be mad at me!"

By now, the woman at the other end of the phone realized the caller had the wrong number. "I'm sorry," she said, "I don't have a daughter named Caroline."

"Oh, Mom! I didn't think you'd be this mad!"

～～～

"I got so little respect, when I was a child—my father carried around the picture of the kid that came with the wallet." Rodney Dangerfield

～～～

A friendly lady encounters a friend with her three grandchildren. She stops to admire them.

"My, what beautiful grandchildren!" she said.

"That's nothing," replied the proud grandmother. "You should see their pictures."

There once was a family named Lambkins
Whose children never learned to use napkins.
They ate, oh so sloppy;
Their lives were unhoppy,
So the Lambkins attached napkins with hat pins.

~~~~~

Tim: I hear you named your sister's children.
Jim: Yes, I named the girl Denise.
Tim: How about the boy?
Jim: Denephew.

~~~~~

Mom: You're not going to school with that lipstick
on your mouth!
Daughter: But, Mom, the teacher is giving me a
make-up exam.

~~~~~

Jack: My little brother stuck his head in our washing
machine.
Jill: What happened to him?
Jack: He got brainwashed.

Why did Daddy Watch leave work early?
He wanted to spend some quality time with his offspring.

~~~~~

Family friend: How's your mom? As pretty as ever?
Kid: Yeah. It just takes her longer.

~~~~~

Mother (on the phone): Come quickly, Doctor! Little Morris just swallowed my fountain pen!
Doctor: I'll be right over. What are you doing in the meantime?
Mother: I'm using a ballpoint.

~~~~~

Did you hear about the family that named the oldest boy Spud? He was a real couch potato.

~~~~~

Mom says Dad gets his exercise by sucking in his stomach every time he sees a pretty lady.

Once there was a child who never spoke. His parents hired famous doctors to examine him, but none could find a reason for his silence. One day when he was eight years old, he plopped down the glass of milk he'd been drinking and said quite clearly, "This milk is sour!"

"But, you can speak!" said his astounded parents. "Why haven't you ever spoken before?"

"Up until now," he said, "everything's been okay."

~~~~~

My wife is such a bad cook that *Gourmet* magazine wants to buy back her subscription.

~~~~~

My daughter took her driving test today. She did a bang-up job!

~~~~~

Junior: Mom, the new baby looks just like Rover.
Mom: Junior, don't say such a thing.
Junior: It's okay, Mom. Rover can't hear me.

Son (on the phone): Mom, hi. How are you? Are you okay?

Mom: Not too good. I've been very weak.

Son: Why are you weak?

Mom: Never mind.

Son: What's wrong?

Mom: Never mind. It's okay.

Son: Why are you weak, Mom?

Mom: I haven't eaten in thirty-eight days.

Son: That's terrible. Why haven't you eaten in thirty-eight days?

Mom: Because I didn't want my mouth to be filled with food if you should call.

~~~~~

Bill Vaughn, in the *Kansas City Star*: "Know what? The trouble with the average family is it has too much month left over at the end of the money."

~~~~~

Son: Ma, I have the largest feet in the third grade. Is it because I'm smart?

Ma: No, son, it's because you're nineteen.

Wife: I just took some pregnancy tests.
Husband: Ha! And what grades did you get?
Wife: A-B-B.

~~~~~

I once had an cuz from Blackheath
Who sat on his pair of false teeth.
He said with a start,
"O dear, bless my heart,
For I've bitten myself underneath!"

~~~~~

College student: Hey, Dad! I've got some great news
for you!
Father: What, son?
College student: Remember that five hundred dol-
lars you promised me if I made the Dean's list?
Father: I certainly do.
College student: Well, you get to keep it.

Hotel guest: Hello, room service. Send up two burned eggs, undercooked bacon, cold toast, and weak coffee.

Room service: Why do you want such a terrible breakfast?

Hotel guest: I'm homesick.

~~~~~

One day a toddler put her shoes on by herself. Her mother noticed the right shoe was on the left foot, so she said, "Honey, your shoes are on the wrong feet."

The little girl looked up at her and said, "But, Mommy, I *know* they're my feet."

~~~~~

Ms. Crocker: This cookbook shows you how to serve your family balanced meals.

Jenny: Oh. I'm already doing that. One day my husband complains, and the next day the kids complain.

Ms. Crocker: Another thing, my dear, when you serve the guests at dinner, be careful not to spill anything.

Jenny: Not me! I won't say a word!

Fern: Oh, I wish I'd listened to my mother.
Ivy: Why? What did she tell you?
Fern: I don't know, I wasn't listening.

~~~~

Heather: How's your son doing at agriculture college?
Mrs. Flower: Great! He so popular, the students voted him most likely to sack-seed.

~~~~

A three-year-old went with his dad to see a litter of kittens. On returning home, he breathlessly told his mom there were two boy kittens and two girl kittens.

"How did you know which were which?" his mom asked.

"Daddy picked them up and looked underneath," the boy replied. "I think it's printed on the bottom."

~~~~

"Everyone thinks their family was rather boring, but mine really was. We had a coffee table book titled *Pictures We Took Just to Use Up the Rest of the Film.*"
Fred Allen

Georgie: Did you come from a big family?
Tory: Mine was a huge family!
Georgie: So how big was it?
Tory: There were so many of us, we had to eat in alphabetical order.

~~~~~

Teenager: Dad, I got a very small scratch on the fender of your new car.
Father: Oh no! Well, let me see. Where is it?
Teenager: In the trunk.

~~~~~

Child: Mom, where were you born?
Mother: In Boston, honey.
Child: How about Dad?
Mother: He was born in Chicago.
Child: And where was I born?
Mother: You were born in California. Why?
Child: Oh, no reason. Just that it's sure lucky we all got together!

Blonde daughter: Dad, what time is it?

Dad: It's 7:15.

Blonde daughter (looking puzzled): You know, Dad, it's the weirdest thing: I have been asking that question to kids at school today, and every time I get a different answer.

~~~~~

Dad: Honey, what is your ambition in life?

Blonde daughter: To be like Vanna White and learn the alphabet.

~~~~~

Frank: Well, Ted, you've certainly come up in the world. You're playing golf with two caddies.

Ted: Oh, it was my wife's idea.

Frank: Your wife?

Ted: Yeah. She thought I ought to spend more time with the kids.

Did you hear about the daughter who spent so much time on the telephone, that when she moved out, the phone company retired her number?

~~~~~

Why can't a woman ask for help from her brother?
He can't be a brother and assist her, too.

~~~~~

Dad: I think Junior's planning to become an astronaut.
Mom: What makes you think so?
Dad: He spends every day sitting in a chair, staring into space.

~~~~~

Billy Joe frantically called the hospital. "My wife's going into labor—you gotta send help!" he cried.

"Relax now," the nurse said calmly. "Is this her first child?"

"No!" Billy Joe replied, "This is her husband!"

What does a son get when he runs over the family parakeet with the lawn mower?
Shredded tweet.

~~~~~

Things you'll never hear your redneck cousin say:

- "I'll take Shakespeare for a thousand, Alex."
- "Duct tape won't fix that."
- "I thought Graceland was tacky."
- "No kids in the back of the pickup; it's not safe."
- "I just couldn't find a thing at Wal-Mart today."
- "Little Debbie snack cakes have too many saturated fats."
- "Elvis who?"
- "Hey, here's an episode of *Hee Haw* that we haven't seen."
- "The tires on that truck are too big."
- "We're vegetarians."

~~~~~

Jerry: I got a practically new BMW for my wife.
Terry: Wow! I'd like to make a trade like that.

Nurse: Why are Mr. and Mrs. Number so happy?
Doctor: They're going to have a little one.

~~~~~

Mrs. Uppity: I'm descended from a very long line. . .
Mrs. Smith: Yes, and your mother should never have
    listened to it.

~~~~~

Rose: When your daughter graduates from college,
    what will she be?
Violet: At this rate, probably about forty.

~~~~~

Maisy: How's your son?
Daisy: Henry's at Harvard.
Maisy: Really! What's he studying?
Daisy: Oh, he's not studying. They're studying him!

~~~~~

Pam: Why did you name your daughter Margarine?
Sam: Because we don't have any but her.

Cliff: You look upset.

Rocky: My son took his driver's test yesterday. He stopped on a dime.

Cliff: Sounds like he passed with flying colors.

Rocky: Not exactly. The dime was in some pedestrian's pocket.

~~~~~

Phyllis: Why do you call your son Flannel?

Dillar: Because he shrinks from washing.

~~~~~

Big sister: Mom says babies are expensive.

Big brother: Yes, but think how long they last.

~~~~~

Wife: I'm home sick.

Husband: But you're at home!

Wife: Yes, and I'm sick of it!

~~~~~

Forecast for mothers-to-be: Showers expected.

Father: I pay your tuition at the Sorbonne, and when I ask you to show me what you've learned, you take me to a fancy restaurant and speak to the waiter in French. You call this a valuable education?

Sam: Sure, Dad. I told him to give you the check.

~~~~~

Wilma: Doris treats her husband like a god.

Betty: What do you mean?

Wilma: Every evening at dinnertime she places a burnt offering before him.

7
For My Lambie Pie:
Jokes about Love and Romance

Father: Davy, your brothers and I think you ought to have a girlfriend.

David: I don't think any girl wants to put up with my flock of sheep.

Father: Perhaps not, but. . .

David: Can you imagine all of us sitting in the balcony at a movie? And what would we see?

Father: Davy, I'm not sure. . .

David: The girls would all want to see a ewe-flick. And the lambs, well I suppose G- or PG-rated films would be okay.

Father: "G?" "PG?" I don't know. . . .

David: Pop, those are the movies that the little ones can see.

Father: Like what?

David: Hmmmm. . .good question.

Daisy: Who was that cute guy I saw you kissing last night?

Maisy: What time was it?

~~~~~

Young Miss Jones: I'm going out with Joe tonight.

Mama Jones: Joe again? If you like his attention so much, why don't you marry him?

Young Miss Jones: Because I like his attention.

~~~~~

What kind of shoes did the plumber wear when he took his girlfriend dancing?

Tap shoes.

~~~~~

Liz: What did the boy egg say to the girl egg?

Phil: Shell we dance?

Liz: Okay. Now, what did the girl cow say to the boy cow?

Phil: What?

Liz: Let's smoooooch.

Did the actress stop dating the movie star?
Yes, he's out of the picture.

~~~~~

What did the snow guy say to the snow gal?
Do you believe in love at frost sight?

~~~~~

What do you call a ghost and a zombie who go out on a date?
Boo-friend and ghoul-friend.

~~~~~

Donald: I hear you broke off your engagement. What happened?

Daisy: Oh, it's just that my feelings for him have changed.

Donald: Are you returning the ring?

Daisy: Oh, no. My feelings for the ring haven't changed.

Did you hear about the woman who put too much mousse on her hair when she was getting ready for a date? She grew antlers.

~~~~~

She: Am I the first girl you ever kissed?
He: Now that you mention it, your face is familiar.

~~~~~

Ann: Did you know that women are smarter than men?
Dan: No, I didn't.
Ann: See what I mean?

~~~~~

Cleo: Officer, that man is annoying me!
Cop: But he's not even looking at you.
Cleo: That's what's annoying me!

~~~~~

Adam: Do you really love me?
Eve: There's no one but you.

Young man: Miss, would you go out with me to-night?
Young woman: I don't go out with perfect strangers.
Young man: I never said I was perfect.

~~~~~

Mickey: Marry me, darling. I know I haven't got buckets of money like my friend Dan, or a hot film career like Dan, or Dan's good looks, youth, terrific sense of humor, or muscles, but I'm loyal and true and I love you.
Minnie: I love you too, honey. . .but first, tell me more about Dan!

~~~~~

What happened after the boy snake and the girl snake got into an argument?
They hissed and made up.

~~~~~

Why were the girls who married Orville and Wilbur happy?
Because they both married Mr. Wright.

What do you call two recently married dandelions?
Newlyweeds.

~~~~~

When two bullets get married what do they have?
BBs.

~~~~~

Why did the cow want a divorce?
Because she had a bum steer.

~~~~~

What would you call a girl with four boyfriends named William?
A Bill collector.

~~~~~

In the first year of marriage, the man speaks and the woman listens. In the second year, the woman speaks and the man listens. In the third year, they both speak and the neighbors listen.

Janey: Aunt Mabel, why is it that you never got married?

Aunt Mabel: Honey, I've got a dog that growls, a parrot that litters the floor, a chimney that smokes, and a cat that stays out late. Why do I need a husband?

~~~~~

Guy: I went out with a nurse last night.

Gal: Well, if you'd behave yourself, maybe they'll let you out without one.

~~~~~

"Marriage is a wonderful institution, but who wants to live in an institution?" Groucho Marx

~~~~~

Boy: Well, I'll see you pretty soon.

Girl: Oh? You don't think I'm pretty now?

The honeymoon period is over when the husband calls home to say he'll be late for dinner, and the answering machine says it's in the microwave.

~~~~

Thelma: What did Miss Muffet say when the spider asked her for a date?
Selma: Ha! No whey!

~~~~

They're a perfect match. Her social life stinks and he doesn't have a scent to his name.

~~~~

How do poets take their wedding vows?
For better or verse.

~~~~

Little Ashley: When I get older, I'm going to marry the boy next door.
Visitor: Why is that?
Little Ashley: 'Cuz I'm not allowed to cross the street.

What did the girl centipede say to the boy centipede at the dance?
You're stepping on my foot. . .my foot. . .my foot.

~~~~~

Frog (telephoning the psychic line): Can you tell my future?
Psychic: You are going to meet a beautiful woman who will be very curious about you.
Frog: That's great. Will I meet her at a party?
Psychic: No, next semester in a biology class.

~~~~~

A college student who had run out of dating funds wrote his father a note:

No money.
Not funny.
Love, Sonny.

His father wrote back:

So sad.
Too bad.
Love, Dad.

Knock, knock
>*Who's there?*
>Amarillo.
>*Amarillo who?*
>Amarillo-fashioned girl.

~~~~~

Jill: Did you hear about the cowboy who married a cowgirl?
Phil: What kind of marriage is that?
Jill: A Western Union.

~~~~~

Dolores: You look exactly like my third husband.
Horace: Is that so? How many times have you been married?
Dolores: Twice.

~~~~~

Bill: Why do you go steady with Melanie?
Will: Because she's different than other girls.
Bill: How so?
Will: She's the only one who'll go out with me.

Betty: You're not going with Bill anymore?
Veronica: I should say not! I put an ad in the personals column and he answered!

~~~~~

What Men Really Mean:

- "Take a break, honey, you're working too hard."
  Really means: "I can't hear the game over the vacuum cleaner."

- "Can I help you with dinner?"
  Really means: "Why isn't it on the table yet?"

- "I missed you."
  Really means: "My socks need washing and we're out of toilet paper."

- "You look terrific!"
  Really means: "Please don't try anything else on, I'm starved."

- "I can't find it."
  Really means: "It didn't fall into my outstretched hands."

- "Do you love me?"
  Really means: "I've done something stupid and you might find out."

- "Do you really love me?"
  Really means: "I've done something stupid and you're going to find out sooner or later."

- "How much do you love me?"
  Really means: "I've done something stupid and someone's on their way to tell you now."

- "She's one of those rabid feminists."
  Really means: "She won't wait on me hand and foot."

- "Honey, we don't need material things to prove our love."
  Really means: "I forgot our anniversary again."

- "That's interesting, dear."
  Really means: "Are you still talking?"

- "That's women's work."
  Really means: "It's difficult, dirty, and thankless."

Bessie: I can't believe you dumped your last boyfriend! That makes seven so far this year.
Tessie: I can't help it. I'm just a curable romantic.

~~~~

Father: Heather, you'll have to send your boyfriend
home earlier.
Heather: Sorry, Dad. Did the noise keep you awake?
Father: No, but the silences did!

~~~~

Attending a wedding for the first time, a little girl
whispered to her mother, "Why is the bride dressed
in white?"

"Because white is the color of happiness, and
today is the happiest day of her life," her mother explained, keeping it simple.

The child thought for a moment, then asked,
"Why's the groom wearing black?"

~~~~

It is true that love is blind, but marriage is an eye
opener.

Cindy: My mother wants me married so badly.
Mindy: Why do you say that?
Cindy: Every time I bring a guy home she measures
    him for a tuxedo.

~~~~

Mick: Why didn't you marry that gorgeous girl you
    were dating?
Keith: Things were going great until I told her about
    my rich uncle. Now she's my aunt.

~~~~

Mrs. Green: My daughter's marrying a military man
    —a second lieutenant.
Mrs. Gray: So, she let the first one get away?

~~~~

Did you hear about the herpetologist who married
the undertaker? They received a lot of monogrammed
Hiss and Hearse towels.

They're a perfect match. She's a vegetarian, and his face is as red as a beet and his hair is as bright as a carrot.

~~~

German boy: Can I have your phone number?
German girl: 999-9999.
German boy: One "no" would have been enough....

8
The Lord Is My Shepherd:
Church and Religion Jokes

Father: I like your new song, Davy.

David: Which one?

Father: You know, "My son is a shepherd, I shall not want."

David: NO, Pop! "The LORD is my shepherd."

Father: Oh, sure. But I was hoping you were going to take care of me in my old age.

David: Dad, listen to the whole song!

If there had been three wise women who went to Bethlehem, they would have asked for directions, arrived on time, helped deliver the baby, cleaned the stable, made a meal, and brought some practical gifts.

～～～

My son recently took up meditation. At least it's better than sitting around doing nothing.

～～～

Harry: In Orthodox Jewish families, it's the man who makes the coffee.
Jerry: Why's that?
Harry: Because the scriptures say, "Hebrews."

～～～

Who are the patron saints of vacations?
St. Thomas, St. Croix, and San Juan.

～～～

What two religions originated in San Francisco?
The Quakers and the Shakers.

Minister: Do you spend much time wondering about the hereafter?
Old-timer: I'll say! Whenever I find myself in front of the refrigerator with the door open, I have to ask myself, "What am I here after?"

~~~~

If Noah were alive today he probably couldn't float a construction loan to build his ark.

~~~~

How does one angel greet another?
She says, "Halo!"

~~~~

Sunday school teacher: Why is it necessary to be quiet in church?
Cute little girl: Because people are sleeping.

~~~~

Pastor: Tell me, Sue, do you pray before you eat?
Sue: No, my mom is a pretty good cook.

Moe: Boy, was I a fat baby!
Joe: Oh yeah? How fat were you?
Moe: I was so fat that instead of baptizing me they
    launched me!

~~~~~

Teacher: Georgie, why did you write in your essay
    that you're Jewish? I happen to know that your
    father is a minister.
Georgie: I can't spell *Presbyterian*!

~~~~~

Reporter: What's that minister doing out there on the ice?
Coach: He's a hockey prayer.

~~~~~

After the christening of his baby brother in church,
little Phil sobbed all the way home in the back seat
of the family car.

Three times his father asked him, "What's wrong?"

Finally the boy replied, "The preacher said he
wanted us brought up in a Christian home, and I
want to stay with you guys."

Noah: Okay, all of you animals, go forth and multiply.
Snakes: Not us.
Noah: And why not?
Snakes: We're adders.

~~~~~

What day do monks get off from work?
Every Friarday.

~~~~~

Minister: So, Bobby, how did you like your first church service?
Bobby: Well, the singing and stuff was okay, but the commercial was way too long.

~~~~~

Abraham decided to upgrade his PC to Windows '95 and Isaac couldn't believe it.

"Dad, your old PC doesn't have enough memory."

And Abraham said, "My son, God will provide the RAM."

Real-McCoy church bulletin announcements:

- "Thursday night: Potluck supper. Prayer and medication to follow."
- "Remember in prayer the many who are sick of our church and community."
- "This being Easter Sunday, Cindy Jones will come forward and lay an egg on the altar."
- "The Rev. Tim Miller spoke briefly, much to the delight of his audience."
- "The church is pleased to have the Rev. Dennis Green as our Advent guest speaker today. His wife Sara accompanies him. After the service we request that all remain in the sanctuary for the Hanging of the Greens."

~~~~~

Why did the Amish couple separate?
He was driving her buggy.

~~~~~

A man going into church was stopped cold by a huge sign the janitor had placed where he had just washed the floor. It read, PLEASE DON'T WALK ON THE WATER.

"The atheists have produced a new Christmas play. It's called *Coincidence on 34th Street*." Jay Leno

~~~~

"I'm lonely," Adam told God in the Garden of Eden. "I need to have someone around for company."

"Okay," replied God. "I'll give you the perfect companion. She is beautiful, intelligent, and gracious—she'll cook and clean for you and never say a cross word."

"Sounds great," Adam said. "But what's she going to cost?"

"An arm and a leg," answered God.

"That's pretty steep," replied Adam. "What can I get for a rib?"

~~~~

Suggested by Leonardo daVinci, what were the last words spoken at the Last Supper?
"Everyone who wants to be in the picture, get on this side of the table."

Milly: Why does your grandmother read the Bible so much?

Lilly: She says that she's cramming for the final exam.

~~~~~

Three possible reasons why Moses led the children of Israel through the wilderness for forty years:

1. God was testing them.
2. God wanted them to really appreciate the Promised Land.
3. Moses refused to ask anyone for directions.

~~~~~

After church on Sunday morning, a young boy suddenly announced to his parents, "Know what? When I grow up I want to be a minister."

"That's fine, son," said his mother. "But what made you decide to be a minister?"

"Well," the boy replied, "I'll have to go to church on Sunday mornings anyway, and I figure it will be more fun if I get to stand up and yell."

Which government agency could St. Peter work for?
The Eternal Revenue Service.

~~~~~

Why did the religious farmer plant prayer books?
He wanted to be a church grower.

~~~~~

What do you call it when a rabbi, a priest, and a minister hold a service together?
A triple pray.

~~~~~

What do you get when a minister owns his own home?
A taxprayer.

~~~~~

What do you call a craft show put on by a monastery?
A friarwork display.

Minister: My new assistant pastor is a real spend-thrift.

Minister's wife: Why do you say that?

Minister: Whenever he's out of town, he calls me parson-to-parson.

~~~~~

Minister: Son, faith can move mountains.

Boy: Yeah, but dynamite's more exciting!

~~~~~

How much fruit did Noah take on to the ark?

Two thousand pears.

~~~~~

Mr. Smith: I'd like to speak to Mr. Jones, please.

Receptionist: Mr. Jones is no longer with us. He's gone to the United Kingdom.

Mr. Smith: I'm so sorry; is it too late to send flowers?

What do you get when you cross a Jehovah's Witness with an atheist?
Someone who knocks on your door for no apparent reason.

~~~~

So the voter says to the politician, "I wouldn't vote for you if you were St. Peter himself!"

To which the politician replied, "If I were St. Peter himself, you wouldn't be in my district."

~~~~

How did Moses part the Red Sea?
He used a sea saw.

~~~~

Why don't Amish people water-ski?
The horses would drown.

~~~~

What's brown and lives in a cathedral in Paris?
The lunch bag of Notre Dame.

What do you call a sleep walking nun?
A roamin' Catholic.

~~~~

Adam and Eve had the perfect marriage. He didn't have to listen to her talk about men she knew before him, and she didn't have to put up with his mother.

~~~~

Did you hear about the New Age church in California?
It has three commandments and seven suggestions.

~~~~

Some more church bulletin goofs:

- "Don't let worry kill you—let the church help."
- "For those of you who have children and don't know it, we have a nursery downstairs."
- "This afternoon there will be meetings at the south and north ends of the church. Children will be baptized at both ends."

Going into church one day, a man looking for a place to sit asked a lady, "Is that seat next to you saved?" To which she replied, "No, but I'm praying for it."

9
Don't Count Your Sheep Before They're Hatched:
Animal Jokes

Father: Davy, remember what your favorite story was when you were a little boy?

David: I sure do, Pop. Noah and his ark!

Father: And?

David: And our silly knock-knock joke. Knock, knock.

Father: Who's there?

David: Noah.

Father: Noah who?

David: Noah a good air freshener that'll work on a boat?

A police dog responds to an ad for work with the FBI. "Well," says the personnel director, "you'll have to meet some strict requirements. First, you must type at least sixty words per minute."

Sitting at the typewriter, the dog types out eighty words per minute.

"Also," says the director, "you must pass a physical and complete the obstacle course."

This perfect canine finished the course in record time.

"There's one last requirement," the director continues, "you must be bilingual."

With confidence, the dog looks up at him and says, "Meow!"

～～～

Customer: Is that pooch a good watchdog?

Pet-store clerk: Absolutely! He'll raise a ruckus every time he sees a stranger.

Customer: How do I know you're not just making that up?

Pet-store clerk: The dog comes with a money-bark guarantee.

The cute little baby snake says to his mother snake, "Mommy, are we poisonous?"

The mommy snake says, "Why do you ask?"

And the baby snake says, "Because I just bit my tongue."

~~~~~

Did you hear about the paranoid bloodhound?
He thought everyone was following him.

~~~~~

Deena: Your bird's making fun of me.
Charlie: Of course he is—he's a mockingbird.

~~~~~

One night an intrepid photographer comes running back to the lodge and announces, "Whew! There was a tiger chasing me all the way across the savannah!"

His wife asks, "Why?"

The photographer says, "I didn't stop to ask!"

What does a well-dressed bee wear to work?
A buzzness suit.

~~~~

Why was Mrs. Rabbit so unhappy?
She was having a bad hare day.

~~~~

Boy sheep: How do you know there is an elephant in front of you at the movies?
Girl sheep: You can't see the screen.

~~~~

Zoologist 1: I just watched a television show about the habits of a family of skunks.
Zoologist 2: Was it a comedy?
Zoologist 1: No. It was a smellodrama.

~~~~

Man: Have you got something to cure fleas on a dog?
Pet-shop owner: I don't know. What's wrong with the fleas?

An alligator walked into a Dairy Queen and ordered a
ice cream cone from the girl behind the counter.
Girl: That'll be five dollars for the cone, sir. By the
way, we don't get many alligators in here.
Alligator: At these prices, I shouldn't wonder.

~~~~~

Mama fish: Don't bite that hook, Junior!
Junior: Why not, Mama?
Mama fish: You're too young to face the reel world.

~~~~~

Zack: Did you hear the police finally caught that cat
burglar?
Mack: What was he doing?
Zack: Purr-owling the neighborhood.

~~~~~

What magazine do cats like to read?
Good Mousekeeping.

Boy Scout: What would you do if a bear came after you while you were hiking through the woods?
Cub Scout: I'd climb a tree.
Boy Scout: That's not smart. Bears can climb trees.
Cub Scout: Not this tree. It would be shaking too hard.

~~~~~

Why do squirrels spend so much time in trees?
To keep away from all the nuts on the ground.

~~~~~

Some old elephant jokes:

- How do you know if there is an elephant under your bed?
Your nose will be touching the ceiling.

- Why did the elephant paint his toenails different colors?
So he could hide in a bowl of M&M's.

- What do you call two elephants on a bike?
Optimistic.

- Why didn't the elephant cross the road?
  He didn't want to be mistaken for a chicken.

- How do you know there's an elephant in your refrigerator?
  Footprints in the butter.

- How do you know if there is an elephant in your bed?
  By the "E" on his pajamas.

- How does an elephant get out of a tree?
  He sits on a leaf and waits for the fall.

- What did Tarzan say when he saw five hundred elephants coming over the hill?
  "Look, there are 500 elephants coming over the hill!"

- What did Tarzan say when he saw five hundred elephants coming over the hill in sunglasses?
  Nothing; he didn't recognize them.

Policeman: You are charged with allowing your dog
    to chase a man on a bicycle.
Man: That's crazy. My dog doesn't even know how to
    ride a bicycle.

~~~~~

What would you get if you crossed an airplane, an
automobile, and a dog?
A flying car-pet.

~~~~~

Camp counselor: Judi, what are you going to do in
    the camp talent show?
Judi: Impressions.
Camp counselor: Good. Let me hear one.
Judi: I love you—ouch! I love you—ouch!
Camp counselor: What's that an impression of?
Judi: Two porcupines kissing.

~~~~~

Where do fish go on vacation?
To Finland.

Two hikers were sitting around a campfire when a huge black bear appeared in front of them.

"Keep calm," said Hiker Pete. "Remember what we read in the book. If you stay absolutely still and look the bear straight in the eye, he won't attack you."

"I don't know about that," said Hiker Jeff. "You've read the book, I've read the book—but has the bear read the book?"

~~~~

Trudy: I'm going on a photo safari in Africa.
Judy: Drop me a lion.

~~~~

A farmer with lots of chickens posted the following sign: FREE CHICKENS. OUR COOP RUNNETH OVER.

~~~~

Why did the homeless turtle cross the road?
To get to the Shell station.

A veterinarian and a taxidermist went into business together. Their slogan: "Either way, you get your precious pet back."

~~~

Teacher: Charlie, what do we call the condition when a snake sheds its skin?
Charlie: Ssss-naked.

~~~

Game warden: What are you doing with that little trout on the end of your line?
Off-season fisherman: Just teaching him to swim.

~~~

What do you get when you cross a teddy bear and a skunk?
Winnie the Peeyew!

~~~

Two lions were strolling down Broadway. One turned to the other and observed, "Not many people around today, are there?"

Where do you see a chorus line of cows?
At Radio City Moooosic Hall.

~~~~~

Chaz: What do you call a parrot in a raincoat?
Snaz: Polyunsaturated.

~~~~~

A tiny turtle began to climb a tree very slowly. Three hours later, it reached the treetop, jumped into the air waving its little front legs, and crashed to the ground. Saved by its shell, the little guy started the process all over again. Five hours later he arrived at the top of the tree, jumped off, waved his little front legs, and fell to the ground. The third time it was the same story.

Two birds were watching from a nest above. The mother bird turned to the daddy bird and asked, "Darling, don't you think it's time we told him he's adopted?"

The Joke's on EWE!

A mouse in her room woke Miss Dowd,
Who was frightened and screamed very loud.
Then a happy thought hit her,
To scare off the critter,
She sat up in bed and mee-owed.

~~~~~

Where does a lion work out?
At the jungle gym.

~~~~~

Why do leopards have spotted coats?
Because the tigers bought all the striped ones.

~~~~~

How do you make bears listen?
Take away their "B" and they're all ears.

~~~~~

What do bees say on hot days?
"Swarm, isn't it?"

A cheerful old bear at the zoo
Could always find something to do.
When it bore him to go
On a walk to and fro,
He reversed it and walked fro and to.

~~~~~

Knock, knock.
Who's there.
Hence.
Hence who?
Hence lay eggs.

~~~~~

Mrs. Goat: I'm expecting a baby.
Mrs. Sheep: Are you kidding?

~~~~~

Mr. Pig: How did you enjoy the buffet?
Mr. Hog: It was swill.

The Joke's on EWE!

Mr. Horse: Did you hear about the swine who bought a million acres of farmland for development?
Mr. Cow: Wow! What a ground hog!

~~~~

What do you call a guy with a seagull on his head?
Cliff.

~~~~

Tim: Why do you have a cow on your front lawn?
Jim: It's mooing the lawn.

~~~~

Farm boy: My pa can't decide whether to buy a tractor or some cows.
City fella: Well, he'd sure look silly plowing his field on the back of a cow.
Farm boy: True, but he'd look even sillier milking a tractor!

A chicken goes into the library and says, "Book," to the librarian.

"You want a book?"

"Book."

"Any book?"

"Book."

So the librarian gives the chicken a novel and off it goes. An hour later the chicken comes back and says, "Book-book."

The librarian says, "Now you want two books?"

"Book-book."

So she gives the chicken two more novels. The chicken leaves, but comes back later.

"Book-book-book"

"Three books?"

"Book-book-book."

So the librarian gives the chicken three books, but she decides she'll follow the chicken and find out what's going on. The chicken goes down an alley, out of town, and toward the woods, into the woods, and down to the river, to the swamp, and there was a bullfrog. The chicken sets the books down by him. The bullfrog looks at the books and says, "Reddit. . . . Reddit. . . . Reddit. . . ."

The Joke's on EWE!

What do you do to a piggy that is bad in class?
Make him sty after class.

~~~~~~

What did the calf say to the haystack?
Are you my fodder?

~~~~~~

Why was the nanny goat so upset?
She had too many kids to take care of.

~~~~~~

Did you hear? The Ace Donkey Rental Company has been accused of providing kickbacks.

~~~~~~

What do you say when a sheep accidentally bumps into a skunk?
Ewe stink.

10
The Lamb Was Sure to Go:
Jokes about School

Father: Any homework tonight, Davy?

David: Yeah, Pop. I've gotta write an essay on sheep education.

Dad: What in the world would that cover?

David: It's letting the sheep know what they didn't even know they don't know.

Teacher: Johnny, did your father help you with your
    homework last night?
Johnny: No, he did it all!

~~~~~

Teacher: If you had one dollar and you asked your
    father for another, how many dollars would you
    have?
Boy: One dollar.
Teacher: Sorry, you don't know your arithmetic.
Boy: You don't know my father.

~~~~~

Little Lily told her mother, "My teacher thinks I'm
going to be famous."

"Oh, really," her mother replied.

"She said all I have to do is mess up one more
time and I'm history!"

~~~~~

Why was the math book so sad?
Because it had so many problems.

When Junior came home after his first day of school, his mother asked, "So, what did you learn?"

"Not enough, they want me to come back tomorrow."

~~~~~

A history teacher had been teaching a lesson about the kings and queens of England. "Do you know who followed Edward VI?" she asked.

"Mary," replied a boy at the back.

"That's right," said the teacher. "And who followed Mary?"

"Her little lamb," said the boy.

~~~~~

Voice (on the phone): Johnny has a cold and can't come to school today.
School secretary: Who is this?
Voice: This is my dad.

An iron worker nonchalantly walked the narrow beam fifteen floors above the city sidewalk. Even though a hurricane was blowing and heavy rain was falling, the worker exhibited no fear and was foot perfect.

When he came down to the sidewalk, a man who had been watching him from ground level went over to him and said, "I was really impressed watching you up there. You were so calm. How did you get a job like this?"

"Well, as a matter of fact," replied the ironworker, "I used to drive a school bus, until my nerves gave out."

~~~~~

Little Johnny: I don't think I deserve an F on this test.
Teacher: I agree, but it's the lowest mark I can give you.

~~~~~

Libby: Dad, I'm going to a party. Would you do my homework for me?
Dad: I'm sorry, honey, it just wouldn't be right.
Libby: Well, maybe not. Give it a try anyway, okay?

Ever wonder if illiterate people get the full value of alphabet soup?

~~~~~~

Teacher: I hope I didn't see you looking at Don's paper.
Pupil: I hope you didn't either.

~~~~~~

Substitute teacher: Are you chewing gum?
Billy: No, I'm Billy Anderson.

~~~~~~

Teacher: Well, at least there's one thing I can say about your son.
Father: What's that?
Teacher: With grades like these, he couldn't be cheating.

~~~~~~

Teacher: Now, if you bought ten apples for ten cents, what would each one be?
Suzy: Rotten! At that price they'd have to be.

A teacher broke up a fight between two boys in the school hallway and took them to the principal.

"Hmmm," said the principal, "who started the fight?"

"I think it was six of one, and a half a dozen of the other," replied the teacher.

"No," protested one of the boys, "there was just the two of us!"

~~~~~

Ferrets live by a code tried and true,
From which humans can benefit, too:
Teach your sons and your daughters
To do unto otters,
As otters would do unto you.

~~~~~

Tommy: Miss Smith, would you punish me for something I didn't do?
Teacher: Of course not.
Tommy: Good, 'cuz I didn't do my homework.

Knock, knock.
Who's there?
Goat.
Goat who?
Goat up on the wrong side of the bed this morning.

~~~~~

Why did the worm oversleep?
It didn't want to caught by the early bird.

~~~~~

Why did the clock get kicked out of school?
Because it was always tocking!

~~~~~

Teacher: Please answer when I call your name—
    Donna Miller.
Willy: Absent.
Teacher: Please, Willy, let Donna answer for herself.

Teacher: What are the last words of the Gettysburg
   Address?
Nate: Er—do you mean the zip code?

~~~~~

What's the favorite subject at the South Pole?
Penguinship.

~~~~~

Mother: The hardest assignment I ever had was to
   write an essay on the belly of a frog.
Daughter: Wow, how'd you get the frog in your
   typewriter?

~~~~~

Why was the little bird punished at school?
It was caught peeping during a test.

~~~~~

Why did the Fig Newton graduate first in his class?
He was one smart cookie.

The children in Miss Sudenga's class were called upon to make sentences with words chosen by their teacher. Miss Sudenga smiled when Tim raised his hand to participate during the challenge of making a sentence with the words *defeat*, *deduct*, *defense*, and *detail*.

Tim stood thinking for a while, all eyes focused on him while his classmates awaited his reply. Smiling, he then proudly shouted out, "Defeat of deduct went over defense before detail."

~~~~

Lisa Marie's dad knew that it was his responsibility to provide religious education to his child, so he regularly read Bible stories to his daughter. One day he read, "A man named Lot was warned to take his wife and flee out of the city, but his wife looked back and was turned to salt."

Lisa Marie asked, "What happened to the flea?"

~~~~

Teacher: Do you know what an echo is?
Ben: Could you repeat the question?

Rosie: I'm learning to speak Spanish.
Tony: At school?
Rosie: No, I'm calling my bank and pressing number 2.

~~~~

Miss Norris was teaching a class in basic math. She confronted little Johnny with a story problem. "If I give you two rabbits and two rabbits and two more rabbits, how many rabbits will you have?"

"Seven," answered Johnny.

"No Johnny," explained the teacher, "that's not the right answer. Let me ask it this way, if I give you two apples, then I add another two apples, and two more apples after that, how many apples have you got?"

"Six," replied Johnny.

"That's right," said his teacher. "So let's try the first one again. If I give you two rabbits, then two more rabbits, and two more rabbits after that, how many rabbits will you have?"

"Seven," was Johnny's answer.

"Seven," replied his teacher, greatly surprised. "How did you get seven?"

"Because I've already got one rabbit at home."

Second-grade teacher Miss Donna was struggling to teach arithmetic to Bobby. Finally she asked, "If you reached into your pants pocket and found a nickel, and then you reached into your other pocket and pulled out another nickel, what would you have?"

Bobby thought a moment, and then replied, "Someone else's pants."

~~~~~

On the first day of school, the kindergarten teacher said, "If anyone has to go to the bathroom, hold up two fingers."

A little voice from the back of the room asked, "How will that help?"

~~~~~

Boy: Isn't the principal a great big dumbbell?
Girl: Say, do you know who I am?
Boy: No.
Girl: I'm the principal's daughter.
Boy: And do you know who I am?
Girl: No.
Boy: Thank goodness!

A first-grade teacher collected old, well-known proverbs. She gave every student in her class the first half of a proverb and then had each one come up with the rest of it. Here are a few samples:

Better safe than. . .punch a fifth grader.

Strike while the. . .bug is close.

It's always darkest before. . .Day Light Savings Time.

Don't bite the hand that. . .looks dirty.

A miss is as good as a. . .mister.

A penny saved is. . .not much.

Two's company, three's. . .the Musketeers.

The pen is mightier than the. . .pigs.

~~~~~

A college student walked into his ornithology class and found five birds with bags over their heads so only their feet could be seen. "What's this?" he asked.

"It's an exam," explained the professor. "Your job is to identify each bird by looking at its feet."

"What a stupid test," complained the student.

"What's your name?" demanded the angered teacher. The student pulled up the legs of his pants and answered, "You tell me."

Cow: What are those lambs over there up to?
Goat: It's a meeting of Gambolers Anonymous.

~~~~~

Where does a pig leave its car when it takes the train?
In a Pork and Ride.

~~~~~

Buyer: Hey, you told me you had purebred police dogs for sale. This animal is the mangiest, dirtiest, scrawniest mutt I've ever laid eyes on. How can you get away with calling him a police dog.
Breeder: He works undercover.

~~~~~

Private hog: Who are you?
Noncommissioned pig: My name is Sergeant Pork and I am an expert in ham-to-ham combat.

Teacher: Billy, name one important thing we have today that we didn't have ten years ago.
Billy: Me!

~~~~

There are three kinds of people—those who can count, and those who can't.

~~~~

Did you hear about the cross-eyed teacher?
She couldn't control her pupils.

~~~~

What did the rooster say when he walked into the cow barn?
"Cock-a-doodle-moo!"

~~~~

Etiquette teacher: What do you say when you come to a door at the same time as a sheep?
Bright student: "After ewe."

Teacher: George, please go to the map and find North America.
George: Here it is!
Teacher: Correct. Now, class, who discovered America?
Class (in unison): George!

~~~~~

Dad: What's the meaning of this F on your essay?
Junior: It stands for *Fantastic*.

~~~~~

Have you heard about Aunt Lillian? She has two or three prescriptions to take, but because she's allergic to cotton, she can't get the pills out of the bottle.

~~~~~

Sheep 1: Baa.
Sheep 2: Moo.
Sheep 1: What's the matter with you? Sheep don't say "moo."
Sheep 2: I'm learning a foreign language.

Teacher: What did the corn chip say to the potato chip?
Class: We don't know.
Teacher: "Hey, let's go in for a quick dip."

~~~~~

Son: I'm too tired to do my homework tonight.
Mom: A little hard work never killed anyone yet.
Son: Right. But why should I risk being the first one?

~~~~~

Class smarty: Why is Six afraid of Seven?
Teacher: I don't know.
Class smarty: Because Seven eight Nine.

~~~~~

Tester: Please name the little streams that run into the Nile.
Janey: The Juveniles?

Aunt Lillian is a neat freak, too. When she adopted a highway, she mopped it once a week. While it was drying, she rerouted traffic with a sign, DON'T DRIVE ON MY CLEAN HIGHWAY.

~~~~~

The lady next door was parading around in her wedding dress. "You must be sentimental," I observed. "Oh no, I'm just far behind in my laundry."

11
Baa Baa! Who's There?
Knock-Knock Jokes

Father: What kind of stories do you tell your sheep, Davy?

David: Well, Pop, they seem to really enjoy satire. The younger ones always enjoy silly puns.

Father: You mean like knock-knock jokes?

David: Yeah, their favorite is:

Knock, knock.
Who's there?
Rubber duck dub.
Rubber duck dub who?
Rubber duck dub, scrub the sheep in the tub.

Father: That's funny, Davy?

David: Pop, you've gotta be a sheep to really get it.

Knock, knock.
Who's there?
Auntie.
Auntie who?
Auntie-disestablishmentarianism. (At one time, one of the longest words in the English language.)

～～～

Knock, knock.
Who's there?
Bing.
Bing who?
Bing of sound mind, I make this my last will and testament.

～～～

Knock, knock.
Who's there?
Barber.
Barber who?
Barber black sheep...

Knock, knock.
Who's there?
Tom Brokaw.
Tom Brokaw who?
Tom Brokaw the good glasses.

~~~

Knock, knock.
Who's there?
Wendy.
Wendy who?
Wendy today, light breezes tomorrow.

~~~

Knock, knock.
Who's there?
Phillip.
Phillip who?
Phillip the tank, the price of gas is going up!

Knock, knock.
Who's there?
Phillip.
Phillip who?
Better phillip the peanut bowl before the game starts on television.

~~~~~

Knock, knock.
Who's there?
Cantilever.
Cantilever who?
Cantilever alone for five minutes before she's into something.

~~~~~

Knock, knock.
Who's there?
Juan.
Juan who?
Juan to get a burger with me?

Knock, knock.
Who's there?
Anita.
Anita who?
Anita new battery for my watch.

~~~~~

Knock, knock.
Who's there?
Candace.
Candace who?
Candice infernal nonsense ever stop?

~~~~~

Knock, knock.
Who's there?
Kareem.
Kareem who?
Kareem and sugar for your coffee?

Knock, knock.
Who's there?
Lettuce.
Lettuce who?
Lettuce in and we'll tell you.

~~~~~

Knock, knock.
Who's there?
Saul.
Saul who?
Saul there is; there ain't no more.

~~~~~

Knock, knock.
Who's there?
Saucer.
Saucer who?
Saucer, but he didn't see me.

Knock, knock.
Who's there?
Altoona.
Altoona who.
Altoona piano, and you play it.

~~~~~

Knock, knock.
Who's there?
Mode.
Mode who?
Mode your lawn yet?

~~~~~

Knock, knock.
Who's there?
Candy.
Candy who?
Candy kids come out and play?

Knock, knock.
Who's there?
Vaughn.
Vaughn who?
Vaughn, two, buckle my shoe.

~~~~

Knock, knock.
Who's there?
Turnip.
Turnip who?
Turnip the music, I can't hear it.

~~~~

Knock, knock.
Who's there?
Al.
Al who?
Al be seeing you.

Knock, knock.
Who's there?
Mustard.
Mustard who?
Mustard been a beautiful baby.

~~~~~

Knock, knock.
Who's there?
Keith.
Keith who?
Keith me quick, thweetheart.

~~~~~

Knock, knock.
Who's there?
Wilbur Wright
Wilbur Wright who?
Wilbur Wright back after this commercial.

Knock, knock.
Who's there?
Dewey.
Dewey who?
Dewey have to listen to these jokes much longer?

~~~~

Knock, knock.
Who's there?
Omelet.
Omelet who?
Omelet smarter than I look.

~~~~

Knock, knock.
Who's there?
Radio.
Radio who?
Radio not, here I come.

Knock, knock.
Who's there?
Ketchup.
Ketchup who?
Ketchup falling star and put it in your pocket. . . .

~~~~~

Knock, knock.
Who's there?
Deena.
Deena who?
Deena is ready.

~~~~~

Knock, knock.
Who's there?
Clark Kent.
Clark Kent who?
Clark Kent come today, he's sick.

Knock, knock.
Whose there?
Tacoma.
Tacoma who?
Tacoma your hair—it's a mess.

12
Thirty Days Hath Sheep-tember:
Seasonal Jokes

Father: You're aware, Davy, that we are living in Old Testament days, right?

David: Sure, Pop.

Father: And that we don't celebrate Christmas or Chanukah yet?

David: I know, Pop.

Father: Then why do I hear your sheep choir singing "Oh Come All Ewe Faithful"?

David: I thought that was better than "While Sheep-herds Washed Their Sox at Night."

Father: Maybe you're right.

Why is March the shortest month of the year?
Because the wind blows a few days out of every week.

~~~~~~

How can a person be five on her last birthday, and seven on her next birthday?
Today's her sixth birthday.

~~~~~~

Melanie: I was born on Flag Day.
Marty: No wonder your hair is so wavy.

~~~~~~

First moth: Have a bite of this delicious sweater, old boy.
Second moth: Sorry, old chap. I've given it up for lint.

~~~~~~

Fanny: What kind of cologne do you wear on March 17?
Annie: Scent Patrick.

Why is the ninth letter of the alphabet like St. Patrick's Day?
Because it's when all the Irish "I's" are smiling.

~~~~

For Police Officer Appreciation Week:

A cop pulls a woman over and says, "Let me see your driver's license, lady."

The woman replies, "I wish you people would get your act together. One day you take away my license and the next day you ask me to show it."

The same cop sees a car weaving back and forth down the highway, and he takes off after it. He pulls up alongside and discovers that the driver is a little old lady who's knitting as she drives. He can't believe it, and he starts yelling at her, "Pull over! Pull over!"

And she hollers back, "No, it's a scarf!"

~~~~

Mort: What's a lumberjack's favorite month?
Snort: Sep-tiiiimberrrrr!

Worried about tax day, a man wrote a letter to the IRS: "I have been unable to sleep knowing that I have cheated on my income tax. I understated my taxable income and am enclosing a check for 150 dollars. If I still can't sleep, I'll send you the rest."

～～～

It goes without saying, the old year takes his leave,
With a beard hanging down to his sleeve.
The kid in the diaper,
Becomes a fussy old griper
In a year—that's so hard to believe.

～～～

Gina: This time of year is good for gossip.
Tina: Why do you say that?
Gina: Because it's time for the winter blah, blah, blahs.

～～～

Why did the pig farmer rush off in such a hurry?
He had to do some last minute Christmas slopping.

What pantomime game do you play on the last Thursday in November?
The Thanksgiving Day charades.

~~~~~

Nick: Have you decided on costumes for the Halloween party?
Nora: Well, since I'm overweight and my husband's crazy, I think we'll go as a horse and buggy.

~~~~~

For Presidents' Day, Leroy observes, "I didn't know George Washington was an orphan."

His teacher replies, "What makes you think he was?"

Leroy answers, "It says in this book he's our country's foundling father."

Leroy's teacher asks, "Was George Washington a sailor or a soldier?"

Little Rosie answers, "He was a soldier."

Her teacher responds, "Right. But how do you know that?"

"Well," said Little Rosie, "I saw a picture of him crossing the Delaware, and no sailor in his right mind would stand up in a boat like that."

Dad: Son, when Abraham Lincoln was your age he walked miles to school every morning.

Son: Yeah? Well, when Lincoln was your age, Dad, he was president.

~~~~~

Father: When Abraham Lincoln lived in Washington, he had a goatee.

Son: Gee, I didn't know they allowed pets in the White House.

~~~~~

Lady: My husband bumped his head at work, and now he thinks he's a giant pecan.

Lawyer: Oh no! Another nut case.

~~~~~

Why don't kangaroos visit Times Square on New Year's Eve?

They're afraid if pickpockets.

Do you know why snowmen get cold feet in bed?
They sleep on sheets of ice.

~~~~~

Why are you shivering so much?
It's the frost day of the week.

~~~~~

How did the Abominable Snowman know he had dandruff?
There were Frosted Flakes on his shoulders at breakfast.

~~~~~

What did the antelope shout on January 1?
Happy gnu year!

~~~~~

Randy: George Washington threw a silver dollar across the Potomac River.
Sandy: I bet he couldn't do that today.
Randy: Why not?
Sandy: A buck just doesn't go as far these days.

Where do Ferris wheels go in October?
To the whirl series.

～～～

On their first wedding anniversary, Mrs. Newly Wed says, "Honey, stop trying to sugarcoat everything that bothers you."

To which Mr. Newlywed responds, "Yes, sweetie."

～～～

For a dude ranch vacation:

Did you hear about the cowboy who was trampled by a flock of sheep?
He dyed-in-the-wool.

～～～

"Halloween was confusing," said little Georgie. "All my life my parents said, 'Never take candy from strangers.' And then they dressed me up in a costume and said, 'Go beg for it.' I didn't know what to do. I'd knock on peoples' doors and say, 'Trick or treat. No thank you.'"

How cold was it?
It was so cold last winter, they had to wait for the phone lines to thaw just to find out what folks had been talking about.

~~~~~

How hot was it?
It was so hot, we had to feed ice cream to the chickens so they wouldn't lay hard-boiled eggs.

~~~~~

At Thanksgiving, my mom always makes too much food, especially one item—like seven or eight hundred pounds of sweet potatoes. There is so much, she has to push them all through dinner and afterwards. She also keeps a running commentary, like, "Did you get some sweet potatoes? : . . They're wonderful. . . . Please notice the little marshmallows. . . . You'll love them. . . . There's more in the oven. . .some more in the garage. . . . The rest are over at the Johnsons'."

While in England on a summer European vacation, a neighbor sent post cards to everyone in her cul-de-sac. Her message read, "Fourth of July is not a big holiday here. The English are still a little testy."

~~~~~

I guess my family was poor. At Easter we didn't have money for a new outfit, so my folks took us to a different church.

~~~~~

Christmas. . .

Why does Santa Claus always go down the chimney?
He'll only do what soots him.

~~~~~

What do you get if you deep fry Santa Claus?
Crisp Cringle.

Mary: Are we going to exchange Christmas presents this year?

Cherry: I don't know about you, but I always exchange mine.

~~~~~

Madge: Did you hear about Fred? He was arrested for doing his Christmas shopping early.

Flora: What do you mean early? It's almost Christmas.

Madge: He shopped before the store was open.

~~~~~

Georgie: I took the kids to pick out a Christmas tree.

Porgie: Was it fir?

Georgie: No, just a few blocks away.

Porgie: No, I mean. . .cedar tree?

Georgie: Well, naturally we cedar tree.

Porgie: No, no! Juniper!

Georgie: Of course not! We paid for it fair and square.

~~~~~

Why does Santa visit his doctor before Christmas?

Because he always gets a flue shot before he slides down chimneys.

What does a deep-sea fisherman send to his friends in December?
Christmas cods.

~~~~~

How does Santa Claus take instant photos?
He uses a North Pole-aroid camera.

~~~~~

Eric and his dad ventured into the woods to bring home a Christmas tree. They walked for hours in the snow, examining every tree they came upon. As the afternoon turned into evening, the temperature dropped ten degrees and the wind began to blow. Still no tree struck their fancy.

Finally Eric piped up, "Listen, Dad, I really think we'd better take the next tree we see, whether it has lights or not."

~~~~~

Why did Santa go to a workshop that builds self-confidence?
Because he no longer believed in himself.

Merri: What did the ghosts say to Santa Claus?

Pickens: "We'd have a boo, boo Christmas without you."

Jack: I work as a substitute Santa at Macy's department store.

Mack: What's your job title?

Jack: Subordinate clause.

~~~~~~

A New York mother took her young son to Gimbels department store to visit Santa Claus.

"What do you want for Christmas, young man?" asked Santa.

"A computer game, a bicycle, and a new basketball," replied the boy.

"I'll do my best to see that you get them," promised the jolly old man.

Later that day the mother took the boy to Macy's, and once again they visited Santa.

"What would you like for Christmas, my little man?" asked the man in red.

"A computer game, a bicycle, and a new basketball."

"And are you going to be a good boy and help your mother?" Santa asked.

The young boy abruptly turned to his mother and said, "Let's go back to Gimbels. I didn't have to make any promises there!"

Mrs. Santa: My husband's good mood gets on my
    nerves sometimes.

Elf: Why?

Mrs. Santa: I asked him to think about something
    beside toys for the kids, so he took up gardening.
    But, guess what—it's "Hoe, hoe, hoe," all over
    again.

~~~~~

For Valentine's Day and weddings:

What's the only way to have your husband remember Valentine's Day?
Celebrate it on his birthday.

~~~~~

A woman rushed up the stairs to the church, late for
the wedding. An usher asked to see her invitation.

    "I don't have one," she said.

    "Well, are you a friend of the groom?" asked the
usher.

    "Certainly not!" she stormed. "I'm the bride's
mother."

"A guy knows he's in love when he loses interest in his car for a couple of days."
Tim Allen

~~~~~

A traffic cop in a small town stopped a motorist for speeding. "But officer," said the driver, "I can explain. . . ."

"Save your excuses," said the cop. "You can cool your heels in jail till the chief gets back."

"But officer. . ."

"Keep quiet!" snapped the cop. "You're going to jail. The chief will deal with you when he gets back."

A few hours later the officer looks in at the prisoner. "Lucky for you that the chief's at his daughter's wedding. It means he'll be in a good mood when he gets back."

"Don't count on it," said the prisoner. "I'm the groom."

~~~~~

Ole and Lena were at the drive-in movie.

Ole: Say Lena, you wanna get in the back seat?

Lena: Naw, Ole, I'd just as soon stay up here with you.

The bride-to-be is with her fiancé, filling out the marriage license form.

Clerk: I see you left some blanks. Hair color. I see you're a blonde.

Blonde: Oh, right.

Clerk: How old are you?

Blonde (counting quickly under her breath): Twenty-two.

Clerk: What is your name?

Blonde (under her breath): "Happy birthday to you. . .happy birthday to you. . .happy birthday, dear *Mandy*."

~~~~~

Why did the two scaries get married?
Because they loved each shudder.

~~~~~

June: Will February March?
Jan: No, but April May.

What did the jar of paste do on January 1?
It made a Glue Year's Resolution.

~~~~~

Why did the homeowner buy a new economy lawn mower this spring?
It got good grass mileage.

~~~~~

What do you get when you cross a summer vegetable with a chicken?
A corny yolk.

13

"Take Me Out to the Baaall Game": Sport Jokes

Father: Are your lambs going to play Little League baseball this summer?

Something David: Oh, I don't know, Pop. Those kids get so upset when they're told to steal a base after their mamas have told them not to take anything that's not theirs....

Young Toby was trying his hand at ice fishing, but was having no luck. Across the ice, Toby saw a guy who was hauling in one fish after another. So Toby went over to the guy and said, "Please tell me your secret for catching all these fish."

"Ee yer erms orm," replied the man.

"What," asked Toby, "are you saying?"

The fisherman tried to speak again, "Ee yer erms orm." Toby still couldn't understand him, so the man spit something out of his mouth and said, "Keep your worms warm!"

~~~~~~

Dad: Son, this tiger hunt marks your passage into manhood. Do you have any questions?

Son: Yes, Dad, if the tiger gets you, how do I get home?

~~~~~~

Footballer 1: Hey guys, help me with this puzzle. Old MacDonald had a what?

Footballer 2: Farm, you dummy!

Footballer 1: Oh, right—farm. How do you spell it?

Footballer 2: E-I-E-I-O.

Salesman: Here, try this new toupee. You can swim,
water-ski, snorkel, or scuba dive with it on.
Bald customer: That's great! I can't do any of those
things now.

~~~~~

Amos: Where did your team end up in the standings?
Andy: In last place, because our batters never got to
hit against our pitchers.

~~~~~

Why don't football players cut their own hair?
Because they can get penalized for clipping.

~~~~~

So, why do I like professional sports so much? Where
else can I *boo* a bunch of millionaires to their faces?

~~~~~

What do you call basketball goals in Hawaii?
Hula hoops.

Why are all tennis players crooks?
They're all racketeers.

~~~~~

Why was the team called a Cinderella team?
They kept running away from the ball.

~~~~~

Why did the baseball player keep ice on his front porch?
Because he wanted to slide home.

~~~~~

Did you hear about the Olympic swimmer who sank all of his money into a swimming pool company and went bankrupt? He got in way over his head.

~~~~~

What job did Dracula Junior have at the baseball park?
He was the bat boy for night games.

Young goalie: But coach, you've just got to pick me! Hockey is my whole life! I live hockey! I dream hockey! I eat hockey!

Coach: Yes, but you can't seem to play hockey!

~~~~~

Dar: I won a bundle at the track on Slowpoke!

Sam: Slowpoke? Why, he came in last in the sixth race.

Dar: Yes, but he was so slow he came in first in the seventh.

~~~~~

Tilly: Who is the most unhappy athlete at a track meet?

Billy: The cross-country runner.

~~~~~

Wife: Where were you going with your golf clubs?

Husband: Would you believe a tee party?

Sue: Do you watch Monday Night Football on your
    television set?
Lou: No. I prefer to sit on the sofa.

~~~~

Why do baseball players always spit on the ground?
Because, if they spit up into the air, it might land on them.

~~~~

Did you hear about the smoochy couple at the golf
club?
They wanted a tee for two.

~~~~

"Baseball is 90 percent mental. The other half is
physical." (Attributed to Yogi Berra)

~~~~

Bill Bounce, being fat for a jockey,
Tried steaming to make him less stocky.
This heated him so
That he had to eat snow,
And change his profession to hockey.

Harry and Barry rented a rowboat for a day of fishing on the lake.

Harry: Yippee, we're doing great! Let's mark this spot so we can come back here another time.

Larry: I already did. See this X I marked on the bottom of the boat?

Harry: You dumbbell! What if we don't get this boat tomorrow?

~~~~~

A golfer was sitting in the clubhouse after playing a round. He looked so upset that a friend went over and asked what was wrong. The golfer said, "It was terrible. On the sixteenth hole I sliced one out onto the freeway and it went through the windshield of a bus, and there was a terrible accident. The bus went out of control and hit a car head-on. I won't even tell you what the results were."

The friend said, "That's awful. What did you do?"

"Well, I closed up my stance and shortened my backswing a little."

Arnold: Did you hear the news?
Sam: What?
Arnold: Golfers aren't using golf clubs any longer.
Sam: They aren't? Why not?
Arnold: Because they're long enough now.

~~~~~

Jockey: My racehorse is named Flea Bag.
Fan: Has he won many races?
Jockey: Nah! He keeps getting scratched.

~~~~~

Fred: Why do you always play golf with Tony? He's
   such a sore loser.
Ted: Because I'd rather play with a sore loser than a
   good winner.

~~~~~

Why did the rubber band go to the baseball game?
He wanted to enjoy the seventh-inning stretch.

Caddy: Sir, you've just aced the eighteenth hole.
Golfer: Wow! That's great!
Caddy: Not really. We're on the fourteenth hole.

~~~~~

Why did the ocean liner sign up for an aerobics class?
It needed to get in shipshape.

~~~~~

How did the busy track star do his homework?
On the run.

~~~~~

What farm animal is the best boxer?
A duck.

~~~~~

How did the karate student feel about failing the test?
He could kick himself.

Sherry: My brother is so dumb.
Terry: How dumb is he?
Sherry: He got a pair of water skis for his birthday.
Terry: So?
Sherry: Now he's looking for a lake with a hill in it.

~~~~~

What do you call a person who does arithmetic and scores touchdowns?
A mathlete.

~~~~~

What did the basketball player ask his fairy god-mother for?
Three swishes.

~~~~~

Coach: What's the difference between a basketball
       player and a dog?
Smarty: The ballplayer wears a uniform, but the dog
       only pants.

Golfer (on the first tee): Before I hire you as my caddy, tell me, are you good at finding lost golf balls?

Caddy: Yes, sir. I'm the best.

Golfer: Great! You're hired! Now go out there and find us some golf balls so we can start the game.

~~~~~

Toddler: Mama, can we go to the racetrack tomorrow?

Mother: Darling, whatever for?

Toddler: I heard on the radio that they're having races for two-year-olds!

~~~~~

Football coach: Tell me, son, what would you do if it were the fourth down with three minutes to play?

Third-stringer: Slide over to the end of the bench where I could see better.

~~~~~

Why are the floors of a basketball court wet?
The players dribble a lot.

Walking down the street, a man was stopped by someone who wanted to sell a talking dog for ten dollars.

The man couldn't believe his ears when the dog said, "Please buy me. I'm a great dog. I played professional football. I was even nominated most valuable player."

"That dog really does talk!" the man gasped. "Why in the world do you want to sell him for only ten dollars?"

"He never played professional football," said the dog's owner, "and I can't stand liars!"

~~~~~

What did the baseball glove say to the baseball?
"Catch you later."

~~~~~

Did you hear the joke about the boxing glove?
It'll knock you out.

~~~~~

Where's the best place to keep your baseball mitt?
In the glove compartment.

"Golf is no longer a rich man's sport. There are millions of poor players." Anonymous

~~~~~

A little boy knocked on the door of a friend's house. When the friend's mother came to the door, the little boy asked, "Can Leonard come out to play?"

"I'm afraid not," said Leonard's mother. "It's still too chilly out, and Leonard has a cold."

"Well, then," said the little boy, "can his football come out and play?"

~~~~~

Screwy: I met someone who is so dumb, he thinks a football coach has four wheels.
Louie: How many wheels does it have?

~~~~~

Gus: Did you hear about the big fight at the bus depot?
Russ: No, what happened?
Gus: Two tickets got punched.

Coach: Freddie, you can be the end, guard, and tackle.

Freddie: That's great, coach!

Coach: Yes, sit at the end of the bench, guard the water bucket, and tackle anyone who gets near it.

~~~~~

The two mountain climbers had reached the end of their exhausting journey. Though at the point of collapse, they made it to the top.

"It almost cost us our lives to climb this mountain," the first climber said, "but it is worth it so we can plant our country's flag on top. This is the proudest moment in my life. Please hand me the flag."

The second climber stared incredulously at him and mumbled, "I thought you had it!"

~~~~~

Father: Well, son, did you make the school football team?

Son: I'm not sure, Dad. The coach took one look at me and said, "This is the end."

What player on a baseball team pours the iced tea?
The pitcher.

~~~~

"Okay, Smith," said the coach, "get in there and tackle 'em."

Smith went into the game. Soon the opposing team was doubled over with laughter. The game had to be stopped.

"What are you doing?" asked the coach. "Why aren't you tackling the other team?"

"Oh—*tackle!*" said Smith. "I thought you said *tickle.*"

~~~~

Father: Now, Michael, don't be selfish. Let your sister have the sled half the time.

Michael: I do, Dad. I have it going downhill and she has it going up.

Jed and Ted decided to explore the countryside on a bicycle built for two. They came to a hill. The going up was hard work, but at last they reached the top.

With short breath and sweating face, Jed said, "That was a pretty tough hill, but we finally made it."

"Yes," added Ted. "Luckily, I had my hand on the brake. Otherwise we would have rolled all the way downhill."

~~~~~

Knock, knock.
Who's there?
Scold.
Scold who?
Scold enough to go ice-skating.

~~~~~

Today in America, a professional wrestler is struck down with a folding chair once every thirty-five seconds—and not once seen by a referee.

Nit: I played hockey last week and broke an arm and leg.
Wit: Some people get all the breaks.

~~~~~

Tony was never an athletic kid. He still remembers the year he was forced to play Little League Baseball by his dad—who was the coach! Halfway through the season, Tony was traded to another family.

Tony's pastor said, "When he was still playing Little League, Tony learned how to steal second. Then he felt so guilty, he'd go back to first."

~~~~~

Stevie Wonder and Tiger Woods were talking, and Stevie said, "Tiger, I've been having trouble with my putting."

Tiger said, "You play golf? But you're blind."

Stevie responded, "I know, but I just have my caddy put a beeper in the hole and I do pretty well. In fact, I'm usually under par."

Tiger said, "Hey, we should play a round sometime."

"Sure, anytime," Stevie agreed. "Pick a night."

A confession: I was ejected from a skating rink today. Evidently they don't allow ice fishing.

~~~~~

A Little League team had just been whipped and the coach told them, "Boys, don't get down on yourselves. You did your best and you shouldn't take the loss personally. Keep your chins up. Your parents are just as proud of you boys as the parents of the girls' team that beat us."

14
Three Bags Full
Jokes about Careers

Father: How are the sheep, David?

David: I think I need to hire an assistant, Pop.

Father: Why's that?

David: I don't have enough time to practice my harp or write new psalms. Chasing these animals around the pasture takes all my time.

Father: We're in agribusiness, Dave, not in the arts. I think you need to settle down and tend to your shepherding.

David: I don't want future generations to think of me only as a sheep chaser.

Father: By the way, Davy, Prophet Samuel wants to stop by this afternoon.

[Read from the Bible, 1 Samuel 16:11-13]

Why did it take the weatherman so long to get dressed for work?
He couldn't find his wind socks.

~~~~~~

Ed: How's your job at the travel agency?
Ned: Terrible. I'm not going anywhere.

~~~~~~

A lawyer is painting his house, and a homeless guy comes around and asks if he can do some odd jobs to make a little money. The lawyer says, "Sure, take a can of paint and go around to the back of the house and paint my porch."

The man does this, and in a few minutes he's back and says he's finished. The lawyer says, "Already?"

"Yeah," the guy replies, "but it isn't a Porsche, it's a Mercedes!"

~~~~~~

Marcy: The weather lady on television said it might snow today.
Darcy: Oh great! Just what this company needs—more flakes!

Elmer: Hear about the glue salesman who became the number one glue salesman in the whole world?

LePage: How'd he do it?

Elmer: He stuck with it.

~~~~

Career lightbulbers:

How many social scientists does it take to change a lightbulb?

They don't change lightbulbs. They search for the root cause as to why the last one went out.

~~~~

How many missionaries does it take to change a lightbulb?

One, and thirty natives to see the light.

~~~~

How many carpenters does it take to change a lightbulb?

None! That's an electrician's job.

How many actors does it take to change a lightbulb?
Only one. They don't like to share the spotlight.

~~~~~

How many consultants does it take to change a lightbulb?
Unknown. They never get past the feasibility study.

~~~~~

How many software people does it take to screw in a lightbulb?
None. That's a hardware problem.

~~~~~

How do you torture an engineer?
Tie him to a chair, stand in front of him, and fold up a road map the wrong way.

~~~~~

How many magicians does it take to change a lightbulb?
Depends on what you want to change it in to.

How many cops does it take to screw in a lightbulb?
Six to sit and hope that it turns itself in.

~~~~~

How many advertising executives does it take to change a lightbulb?
Interesting question. What do you think?

~~~~~

How many psychiatrists does it take to change a lightbulb?
One, but only if the lightbulb wants to change.

~~~~~

Hypochondriac: Doctor, am I going to die?
Doctor: That's the last thing you're going to do.

~~~~~

Doctor: What seems to be the matter?
Patient: I have a sore throat, I ache, and I have a fever.
Doctor: Sounds like you have some sort of a virus.
Patient: Everyone in my office has it.
Doctor: Aha, sounds like a staff infection.

Patient: Doctor, you've got to help me; I can't stop thinking I'm a goat.
Doctor: I see. And how long have you had this problem?
Patient: Ever since I was a kid.

~~~~~

Before they decide what kind of lumber to use on a house, carpenters usually get together and have a board meeting.

~~~~~

Consultant: Why did you buy that bottled-water plant?
Businessman: I believe in having liquid assets.

~~~~~

"I think I'm a moth."
"I think you need a psychiatrist."
"I know."
"So, why did you come in here to a gas station?"
"The light was on."

Show me a celestial body that goes into footwear. . .
and I'll show you a shoe business star!

~~~~

Jack: What do you do for a living?
Bob: I sell boats.
Jack: Motor boats?
Bob: No, I'm in charge of sails.

~~~~

What happens to good hairdressers?
They dye and go to heaven.

~~~~

Heard about the guy who had to quit his job due to ill-
ness and fatigue? His boss was sick and tired of him.

~~~~

Ted: What do you do for a living?
Fred: I'm a censor.
Ted: You must be the type of guy who sticks his no's
     in everybody else's business.

Man: You really should let Joe represent you in this lawsuit.

Lady: Joe! Why, he graduated at the bottom of his law-school class. I don't think he ever won a case.

Man: True, but he'll lose for you cheaper than anyone else in town.

~~~~

Huey: So, you're a night watchman. What do you watch?

Dewey: I don't know. It's so dark I can't see a thing.

~~~~

In an elevator:

Passenger: I guess your job has its ups and downs, heh, heh.

Elevator operator: I don't mind the ups and downs. It's the jerks I can't stand!

~~~~

Diner: Ask the chef if he has pig's feet?

Waiter: Not me. I need this job.

Do you have to be smart to work in a perfume factory?
No, but you need good scents!

~~~~

Suzi: Working at this company is a real rat race.
Salli: What can we do about it?
Suzi: Well, first we're going to strike for more cheese.

~~~~

Customer: I'd like three dozen of these lovely anemones.
Florist: I'm sorry, we only have a dozen left. How about letting me add these lovely ferns? They'll make a spectacular arrangement.
Customer: They certainly will—I'll take them. With fronds like these, who needs anemones?

~~~~

Donna: How's that brother of yours?
Lisa: He's climbing the ladder of success.
Donna: How nice. I suppose he's on Wall Street, or in advertising. . . ."
Lisa: No, actually, he's a house painter.

Bud: Whatever happened to that bald barber?
Lou: He departed.

~~~~~

It was Sunday when the brain surgeon discovered a huge leak in his basement pipe. He rushed upstairs and called the plumber.

"Acme Plumbing? This is an emergency! Get over here quick!"

"Okay, but I charge extra for Sunday emergency service," explained the plumber.

"Anything! Just stop this leak!"

The plumber arrived, took out a tiny wrench from his canvas bag, and lightly tapped the pipe. The leak stopped. Then the plumber handed the relieved homeowner a bill for five hundred dollars.

"What?" screamed the surgeon. "That's unbelievable! Why, I'm a brain surgeon and I don't make five hundred dollars for five minutes of work!"

"I know," agreed the plumber. "Neither did I when I was a brain surgeon."

Patient: I'm a little nervous, Doc. This is my first operation.
Doctor: Mine, too.

~~~~~

Bookstore clerk: May I help you?
Book lover: I'm just browsing.
Bookstore clerk: Well, high browse is to the left; low browse is to the right.

~~~~~

Patient: Doctor, I don't know what's wrong with me— I hurt all over. If I touch my shoulder here, I hurt, and if I touch my leg here, I hurt, and if I touch my head here, I hurt, and if I touch my foot here, I hurt."
Doctor: I believe your finger is broken.

~~~~~

Darcy: How was your day at work, dear?
Jason: Just great! My boss told me I should try to see the big picture, so I spent the afternoon at the movies.

Employee 1: Ouch!
Employee 2: What happened?
Employee 1: I sliced my finger with the edge of my check.
Employee 2: Now that's a real pay cut!

~~~~~

Census taker: And how many people work in your factory, sir?
Factory owner: I'd say about one out of ten.

~~~~~

Daryl: I've hired a carpenter who hammers like lightning.
Tim: He's that fast?
Daryl: No, he never hits the same place twice.

~~~~~

What do you get if you cross a native of Maine with a cartoonist?
A Yankee Doodler.

The foreman laughed when a tiny old man in a plaid shirt applied for a job as a lumberjack.

"So you think you can be a lumberjack? What's your experience?" asked the foreman.

"I've felled a million trees single-handedly," said the old man. "Ever hear of the Mojave Forrest?"

You mean the Mojave Desert," corrected the foreman.

"Sure—now!"

~~~~

Fran: I used to work at a factory that made chairs. The wages were low, but we forced them to raise our pay.
Ann: How did you do that?
Fran: We staged a sit-down strike.

~~~~

Show me a farmer who raises sheep for their wool. . . and I'll show you a shear cropper.

A young businessman had just started his own firm. He rented a beautiful office and had it furnished with the very best. Sitting at his fancy desk, he saw a man come into the outer office.

Wishing to appear busy to his potential first customer, he picked up the telephone and improvised a one-sided conversation with a big spender. He threw big figures around and made giant commitments. Finally he hung up and asked the visitor, "May I help you?"

The man answered, "Sure, I've come to install that phone!"

~~~~

Responses to the question, "How's your job at the riding academy?"

"I'm saddled with a lot of work."
"I never have a free run."
"People ride me at work."
"The bucks aren't that good."
"I never get to horse around."

The old family physician took his son into partnership after the young man received his medical degree. The old doctor then went off on a two-week vacation, his first in years.

When he got home, he asked his son if there'd been any problems at the clinic. The son said no, everything went well. "In fact," he said, "you know that rich old widow, Mrs. Ferguson? I cured her of her chronic indigestion."

"Well, that's fine," said the old doctor. "But Mrs. Ferguson's indigestion is what put you through medical school."

~~~~~

Show me a coal miner who wears a flashlight on his helmet, and I'll show you a guy whose work makes him lightheaded.

The Joke's on EWE!

A dentist named Archibald Moss
Fell in love with the dainty Miss Ross.
But he held in abhorrence
Her Christian name, Florence,
So he renamed her his Dental Floss.

15

"A Sheep in Sheep's Clothing":
More Favorites

Father: Read this, Davy. It's by a man named Grosse.

David: Let's see, Pop. "We have all heard of a wolf in sheep's clothing, well I want to suggest that we have some sheep in sheep's clothing out in our fields."

Father: What do you think that means, son?

David: I think Mr. Grosse is trying to tell us to help our sheep to develop a sense of humor.

Father: How in the world can a sheep have a sense of humor?

David: Pop, you ought to hear the flock laugh at the jokes that follow. These are some of their favorites. . . .

Mel: I can't take good photos because I can't concentrate on my subjects.

Nell: If you want to be a successful photographer, you've got to learn to focus.

~~~~~

In the days of the Berlin Wall, there was a little old man who crossed the checkpoint every week, pushing his bike and carrying a heavy sack. The border guard, suspecting him of smuggling, always searched the sack thoroughly but never found anything worthwhile.

One day, after the wall came down, the guard ran into the little old man.

"Look, I just know you were smuggling something all those years but I could never prove it," said the guard. "Tell me what it was."

The little old man chuckled and said, "Bicycles."

~~~~~

Tim: What do you do for a living?

Jim: I work with figures.

Tim: Accountant?

Jim: No. Fitness instructor.

Why did Adam get the first fig leaf?
Because he wore the plants in the family.

~~~~~

Fern: I just can't eat the way I used to without gaining weight.

Ivy: My husband eats like a horse and weighs just what he weighed twenty years ago—350 pounds.

~~~~~

What did Paul Revere say when he finished his famous ride?
Whoa!

~~~~~

Patty: The cow just got married.
Matty: I guess that makes her a honeymooer.

~~~~~

Guard: Nice suit, boss. Did you buy it off the rack?
Warden: No. It's jailer made.

What do Sir Galahad and Sir Lancelot watch at six o'clock?
The Knightly News.

~~~~~

What do you get when you put overweight sheep in a steam room?
Wool sweaters.

~~~~~

Orange: You'd better get off of the beach.
Banana: Why?
Orange: You're starting to peel.

~~~~~

Why did the alga and the fungus get married?
They took a lichen to each other.

~~~~~

Did you hear about the couple that was so poor, she fixed Hamburger Helper with no hamburger?

From a middle school essay:

"Poets are imaginative people. They imagine people listen to their poems. There isn't much money in writing poetry, but first you must be completely dead."

~~~~~~

Ever since he graduated from high school, Brian spent most of his waking hours stretched out on the couch watching sports programs and eating snacks. One day, as he reached for another Twinkie, he fell off the sofa onto his head and had to be rushed to the hospital. After x-rays were taken, the doctor went right to Brian's bedside.

"I'm sorry, but I have some bad news, young man. Your x-ray shows that you've broken a vertebra in your neck. I'm afraid you'll never work again."

"Thanks, Doc. Now what's the bad news?"

~~~~~~

Toni: I've discovered that men don't like perfume that smells like flowers.
Lisa: So what kind do you wear?
Toni: It's called "New Car Interior."

They're a perfect match: He's a chiropractor and she's a pain in the neck.

~~~~~

Lady: Why is my mail so soggy?
Postman: Postage dew.

~~~~~

What's the difference between Goldilocks and a genealogist?
A genealogist is interested in forebears.

~~~~~

A man approached the sales counter of an auto-parts store. "Excuse me," he said. "I'd like to get a new gas cap for my Yugo."

"Sure," the clerk replied. "Sounds like a fair exchange."

Knock. Knock.
Who's there?
Fur!
Fur who?
Fur the last time—open the door!

~~~~

Calvin: Is it very windy?
Alvin: No, I always have trouble keeping my eye-
brows on.

~~~~

The businesswoman ordered a fancy floral arrangement for the grand opening of her new store, and she
was furious when it arrived adorned with a ribbon
which read, MAY YOU REST IN PEACE.

Apologizing profusely, the florist got her to calm
down with the reminder that in some funeral home
stood an arrangement bearing the words GOOD
LUCK IN YOUR NEW LOCATION.

Airy: What's the difference between an umbrella and a pickle?

Harry: You're making this riddle up?

Airy: Yes.

Harry: What's the difference between an umbrella and a pickle? Hmmm… I give up.

Airy: Oh? I give up, too.

Harry: I thought you said that you make up riddles.

Airy: I do. I make up riddles. I don't make up answers.

~~~~~

A reminder: If you don't go to people's funerals, they won't come to yours.

~~~~~

There once was a lady name Lynn
Who was so uncommonly thin,
That when she assayed
To drink lemonade,
She slipped through the straw and fell in.

A guy in a spelling bee was asked to spell Mississippi. "Which," he asked, "the river or the state?"

~~~~~

Two truck drivers came to a low bridge. The clearance sign said 10 FEET 8 INCHES. When they got out and measured their truck, they discovered their vehicle was eleven feet. The first man looked at the other and said, "I can't see any cops around. Let's go for it!"

Bumper Stickers:
- EVACUATE THE ROAD—STUDENT DRIVING.
- I IS A COLLEGE STUDENT.
- A HUSBAND IS SOMEONE WHO TAKES OUT THE TRASH AND GIVES THE IMPRESSION THAT HE JUST CLEANED THE WHOLE HOUSE.
- HUG YOUR KIDS AT HOME AND BELT THEM IN THE CAR.
- SPELL-CHECKERS ARE HEAR TWO STAY.
- AMBIVALENT? WELL, YES AND NO.
- I HAVEN'T LOST MY MIND—IT'S BACKED UP ON A DISK SOMEWHERE.
- PROCRASTINATE NOW!

- MY WIFE KEEPS COMPLAINING I NEVER LISTEN TO HER—OR SOMETHING LIKE THAT.
- TRUST IN GOD—BUT LOCK YOUR CAR.
- PRESERVE NATURE—PICKLE A SQUIRREL.
- WEAR SHORT SLEEVES—SUPPORT YOUR RIGHT TO BARE ARMS.
- CAUTION! DRIVER APPLYING MAKEUP.

~~~~~

Hank drained all the water out of his swimming pool.

"Why did you do that?" asked Frank.

Hank answered, "I want to practice diving, but I can't swim."

~~~~~

Lena: My two specialties are meatballs and peach pie.

Ole: I see. And which one is this?

~~~~~

Tarzan came home from a hard day's work and announced, "Jane, it's a jungle out there!"

I went down the street to the twenty-four-hour grocery store. When I got there, a guy was locking the front door. I spoke up, "Hey, the sign says you're open twenty-four hours." The guy said, "Yes, but not in a row."

~~~~~

A certain bathroom-scale manufacturer was very proud of the new model being introduced at the trade fair. "Listen to these features: It's calibrated to one one-hundredth of a pound; it can measure your height, as well, in feet or meters; it gives you a readout via an LED or human voice simulator; and that's not all. . . ."

"Very impressive," interrupted a not-too-slender home-furnishings sales rep, "but before I place an order I'll have to try it out."

"Be my guest," said the salesman.

But no sooner had the sales rep stepped on the scale than a loud, very human-sounding voice issued forth: "One at a time, please, one at a time."

~~~~~

How do you know when a computer illiterate's been using your laptop?
There are eraser marks on the screen.

A woman stormed into a home-furnishings shop. "I have come to return this rug which I bought from you last week. You promised me that it was in mint condition."

"So it is, madam," explained the shop manager. "Look at the hole in the middle."

~~~~~

My doctor tried kidnapping for a while, but nobody could read the ransom notes.

~~~~~

A city slicker walks into the hardware store to buy a chainsaw. He announces, "I want one that will cut down about ten trees in an hour." So the clerk sells him one.

The next day the city slicker comes in all upset and says, "Hey, this chainsaw only cut down one little tree in one hour!"

The clerk replies, "Gee, let me take a look at it."

He pulls the starter rope, the saw starts up, and the slicker asks, "What's that noise?"

Patient: Doctor, I have this terrible problem. I think I'm a dog: I walk around on all fours, I keep barking in the middle of the night, and I eat dog food.

Doctor: Very interesting. Lie down on the couch, please.

Patient: I'm not allowed on the couch.

~~~~~

What do Alexander the Great and Winnie the Pooh have in common?
They have the same middle name.

~~~~~

Why do firehouses have dalmatians?
To help them find the hydrants.

~~~~~

Why is a moon rock tastier than an earth rock?
Because it's a little meteor.

What did number 0 say to number 8?
Nice belt.

~~~~~

What does a dog do that a man steps into?
Pants.

~~~~~

In high school my sister went out with the captain of the chess team. My parents loved him. They figured that any guy who took that long to make a move was okay with them.

~~~~~

What happened to the survivors of a collision between a red ship and a blue ship?
They were marooned.

~~~~~

What do you get if you divide the circumference of a pumpkin by its diameter?
Pumpkin pi.

A city guy was touring the country when he came across an old farmer sitting on a tree stump and idly chewing a blade of grass.

"How's things?" asked the tourist.

"Can't complain," said the farmer. "I had some trees to cut down, but a cyclone came along and spared me the trouble."

"Well, you know what they say about an ill wind."

"Then a lightning storm set fire to the brush pile and saved me the trouble of burning it."

"Another stroke of luck. What are you going to do next?"

"Oh, nuthin' much. Just waiting for an earthquake to come along and shake them potatoes out of the ground."

~~~~~

What do you get when you cross a snowman with a vampire?
Frostbite.

A debt collector knocked on the door of a house and asked, "Is Jim here?"

The woman who answered the door said, "No, Jim has gone for cotton."

The next day, the debt collector tried again and once more was told that Jim wasn't in because he had gone for cotton.

So he tried the following day and again was told, "Jim has gone for cotton."

Then on the fourth day, the woman told him, "Jim died yesterday."

Thinking he was being tricked, the debt collector went to the local cemetery to find out whether Jim really had died. Then he saw it—there on the man's tombstone, it read, JIM. GONE NOT FOR COTTON.

~~~~~

Everything you've ever wanted to know about sheep:

Where do sheep take a bath?
In a baaath tub.

What do you get when you cross a sheep with a porcupine?
An animal that can knit its own sweaters.

~~~~~

Why did the sheep get arrested?
She made a ewe turn.

~~~~~

Mary had a little lamb,
It ran into a pylon.
Ten thousand volts went through his bod,
And turned his wool to nylon.

~~~~~

How do sheep greet each other at Christmas?
"Merry Christmas to ewe."

~~~~~

What do you call a sheep that's always quiet?
Shhhhhheep.

The Joke's on EWE!

Where does a sheep get a haircut?
It goes to a baaa-baaa shop.

~~~~

Freddy: Little lamb, can you come outside and play?
Little lamb: No, I've been baaaaad.

~~~~

Did you hear about the lamb who called the police?
He had been fleeced.

~~~~

How can you tell when sheep go bad?
They become ewesless.

~~~~

How are sheep elected president?
Ewe-nanimously.

What happened to the clock that fell into the sheep dip?
It lost all its ticks.

~~~~~

What would you get if you crossed a goat and a sheep?
An animal that eats tin cans and gives back steel wool.

~~~~~

What do you get if you cross a boa and a sheep?
A wraparound sweater.

~~~~~

How many sheep does it take to knit a sweater?
Don't be silly; sheep can't knit.

~~~~~

Pam: My dog ate a whole ball of wool!
Sam: What happened?
Pam: Her puppies were all born wearing socks.
Sam: That's some yarn.

What song did the Ames Brothers make famous?
"Ewe, Ewe, Ewe, I'm in Love With Ewe, Ewe, Ewe."

~~~~~

What do you call a sheep without legs?
A cloud.

~~~~~

What sheep has a river named after her?
The Ewe-phrates.

~~~~~

What do you call a dancing sheep?
A baaaa-larina.

Add Your Favorite Jokes

_____

_____

_____

_____

_____

_____

_____

_____

_____

_____

_____

_____

_____

_____

_____

_____

_____

_____

_____

_____

_____

Other Joke Books from
Barbour Publishing

NOAH'S FAVORITE ANIMAL JOKES
Jennifer Hahn
Categorized by animal—this book is packed with hilarious, crazy, and/or corny stories, riddles, and one-liners appropriate for anyone. 240 pages
1-58660-995-5

THE TEACHER, TEACHER JOKE BOOK
Jennifer Hahn
With hundreds of jokes from elementary, junior high, high school, college—even Sunday school—this collection is sure to bring back memories and make you laugh. 240 pages
1-59310-138-4

THE WORLD'S GREATEST COLLECTION
OF CHURCH JOKES
Paul M. Miller
This hilarious collection contains scores of funnies—involving pastors, deacons, Sunday school teachers, pew sitters, and kids—all of them clean, funny, and good-natured. 256 pages
1-59310-018-3